APHRA BEHN

APHRA BEHN
Selected Poems

*edited with an introduction
and notes by Malcolm Hicks*

Fyfield*Books*

First published in 1993 by
Carcanet Press Limited
208-212 Corn Exchange Buildings
Manchester M4 3BQ

A CIP catalogue record for this book
is available from the British Library.
ISBN 1 85754 017 4

The publisher acknowledges financial assistance
from the Arts Council of Great Britain.

Set in 10pt Palatino by Bryan Williamson, Frome
Printed and bound in England by SRP Ltd, Exeter

Contents

Introduction

The growing rehabilitation of 'the excellent Madam Behn', the incomparable Astraea',[1] is part of the general development of interest in women's writing that has occurred in recent years, and done so much to restore or establish reputations. But it would be wrong to suppose that Aphra Behn's advancement has involved some form of special pleading. In the second half of the seventeenth century she was considered a worthy contemporary of male poets and dramatists who have not suffered the same eclipse. (Her comparable qualities as a writer of prose fiction might also be mentioned, but she was first in the field in that genre and lacked immediate competitors.) She had to fight to defend her corner in a robustly male chauvinist world, where both sexes derided the notion that any woman should scorn the modesty of her nature and compose original works in order to earn a living. It is this taint of immodesty that hung about her life and the boldness of her writings, and helped to confuse the judgements of later ages.[2] An inventory of injustices would have the effect of seeming to protest too much in her favour, so one Victorian instance might stand as example. In a book entitled *English Poetesses: a series of critical biographies with illustrative extracts* (1883), the author grudgingly introduces Aphra Behn as follows:

> It is a pity, almost, that the next name must have a place accorded it; certainly a pity that beside any records of what the more exalted spirit of woman has achieved, mention should be made of so unsexed a writer as Mrs. Aphra Behn. Yet she was a woman, writing much that was vigorous and a little that was poetical, and so must needs be catalogued among the verse writers with whom it is the business of these pages to deal.[3]

Echoing Shakespeare, the writer hints that Aphra Behn is as 'unsexed' in her own way as Lady Macbeth, when she wilfully renounces all the instinctive, or customary, attributes of womankind in her own and her husband's incitement to regicide. (Behn, incidentally, was a staunch royalist.) An author who is firmly, if vaguely, in favour of the 'exalted spirit of woman', who opposes the 'vigorous' against the 'little that was poetical', betrays a representative taste which was incapable of appreciating Behn's candid yet subtle explorations of relationships between the sexes from a female point of view.

At this juncture, a latter-day authority should be summoned. In her invaluable *Aphra Behn: An Annotated Bibliography of Primary and Secondary Sources* (1986), Mary Ann O'Donnell concludes her general introduction with the impassioned comment that 'It is time to restore to Aphra Behn the Fame she longed for, the Fame she worked for, the Fame she deserves – not because she is a woman writer but because she is an important writer.'[4] Contemporary critics are beginning to respond, but the principal concern so far has been biographical, not least because Aphra Behn led such an intriguing life. Inspired guesswork, developed out of a painstaking search for the facts of her career, has created a series of possibilities that is too complex to be detailed here.[5] Maureen Duffy may be correct in proposing that Aphra Behn was one Eaffry Johnson, baptized on 14 December 1640 at St Michael's Harbledown, just outside the city of Canterbury, although both O'Donnell and Jane Jones insist that the evidence so far discovered is insufficient to establish the point. Her apparent adoption into the Culpeper family, where her mother seems to have served as wet nurse to the late Sir Thomas Culpeper's son of the same name, gives the earliest indication of formative experience which led to a lifelong acquaintance with the (Tory) gentry, and to fierce royalist loyalties. Jones has reaffirmed earlier biographers' contentions that Behn was the daughter of a well-to-do barber, who as a girl would have enjoyed life in a cosmopolitan Canterbury. As a young woman she seems to have voyaged to Surinam, a colony on the north-east coast of South America, where her father would have taken up the office of Lieutenant General but for dying *en route*. Behn's putative residence there has been dated to the winter of 1663-64; and would have furnished her with material for her novel, *Oroonoko*, the one work which has helped to sustain her literary reputation from her own times to ours. 'No record of [her] marriage has been found, and there is no evidence about the fate of Mr Behn', Jones reminds us,[6] but two shadowy contenders for her hand have been conjectured: a virile young sea captain, possibly a Dutchman, who might have perished on the main; and an ageing merchant of Dutch extraction, who might have died in London in the plague year of 1665. Whatever the case, Behn's husband never comes to prominence. Better documented is her subsequent employment in espionage. She was dispatched on a mission to Antwerp in August 1666, to try to persuade one of the disaffected Englishmen living there, William Scot – son of the regicide, Thomas Scot, who had been put to death for his part in the execution of Charles I – to turn double agent and supply information on both the Dutch, with whom the English were frequently at war in the 1660s, and his own anti-royalist countrymen. In her 'A Pastoral to Mr. Stafford [etc.]', published in the *Miscellany* of 1685, under the guise of Amarillis, Behn speaks these lines:

> Once, Thirsis, by th' Arcadian King's commands,
> I left these shades, to visit foreign lands;
> Employed in public toils of state affairs,
> Unusual with my sex, or to my years; . . .
>
> (ll.71-4).

Behn's name could have been put forward by her 'foster-brother' Culpeper, or by Thomas Kiligrew, politician and manager of the King's Company at the Theatre Royal in Drury Lane, to Lord Arlington, the head of Charles II's intelligence service. Despite her earnest pleadings for redress, Behn failed to be paid for her endeavours. She managed to get back to England in distressed circumstances, only to be threatened with debtor's prison on return to London in May 1667. Whether she was compelled to some form of prostitution in order to survive, or submitted to being a kept woman, it is from this period that we can date her first writing for a living. She might well have begun copying and editing in the late 1660s, while her theatrical career was initiated in 1670 (possibly 1669) with the production of *The Forced Marriage* by the Duke's Company at the Playhouse in Lincoln's Inn Fields. She wrote verse all her life, but the publication of her three miscellanies of poetry, as well as her occasional poems, all date from the 1680s. It seems that Behn was obliged to develop her abilities in poetry, fiction and translation when she returned to publishing after a break of at least a year in 1684. A warrant had been issued for her arrest following her bold satire on the Duke of Monmouth's rebellion against his royal father, Charles II, in the epilogue to an anonymous play called *Romulus and Hersilia* in 1682. Although she escaped with a caution, it is quite possible that the disillusioned dramatist was for some time denied access to the theatres. She might have found it politic to travel abroad, possibly to Italy, until the storm blew over. Her problems would have been exacerbated by the fact that the two licensed companies had joined forces in 1682, revivals were in fashion, and fewer new plays were required. Progressively incapacitated in her final years (she found it increasingly difficult to get about and to hold a pen even), beset with financial anxiety, socially isolated and dismayed by the political turn of events which had removed James II from the throne, she died on 16 April 1689, and lies buried in the east cloister of Westminster Abbey.

If Behn's biographers have been a little too eager to flesh out the life, they have excelled in providing the social, cultural and political context in which to appreciate its achievements and conflicts. What has been lacking is a body of sustained critical attention to the works themselves 'hampered by the inadequacy of available texts'. Until very recently, the reader has had to search out Montague Summers' pioneering six-volume edition of 1915 (reprinted 1967).[7] Where the poetry is concerned, it is unfortunate that Summers chose to exclude Behn's substantial political poems, or poems on affairs of state. It is difficult to see why, for he ranks them highly;[8] and although it would be wide of the mark to detect in their omission some patriarchal reservations about a woman who presumed to pronounce so grandly on political affairs (the plays he prints are full of political allusions), some form of bias does seem to have crept in to Frederick Link's book-length study of Aphra Behn, which O'Donnell notes as the 'most thorough critical survey of Behn's works available'.[9] Link concludes that the 'substantial poems Mrs Behn produced for great occasions have been largely forgotten and do not merit revival'. He would salvage only that 'handful of exquisite lyrics, slight as they are, [which] have proved less ephemeral: it is owing to them and to her prologues and epilogues that she may claim a place as a minor Restoration poet'.[10] This is scarcely an advance on the Victorian judgement quoted earlier, and takes its place in a history of critical appraisal which has proved as insidious as it is eminent.

That master lyricist, Swinburne, astutely compared Behn to William Blake (and Villon) in his study of Blake first published in 1868. Her verse possesses 'some real energy of beauty and form' and 'a noble sense of metre to be found in no other song writer of her time'.[11] No compiler of a selection of Behn's poetry would wish to disagree, but would insist that the range of excellencies is not confined to song-writing. In her evocation of an unfettered golden age, Behn broadly shares Blake's championing of innocence against the restraints of experience. This attitude frequently underwrites the argument, wit and diplomacy of her complimentary addresses and elegies, and her poems addressed to both men and women where she acutely charts the complex encounters between the sexes. From the complaints of the sixteenth century followers of Petrarch onwards, English poetry abounds in male protests at cruel mistresses or, in happier (but more tedious) vein, male eulogies to mistresses' eyebrows. The sex is not incapable of clever simulations of the female perspective, of course, just as Behn herself can encompass the male point of view, but in her poetry it is so stimulating to encounter frank and sensitive appraisals from a woman's vantage – or, perhaps one should say on occasions, disadvantage – point. Vehemently opposed to the disingenuousness of conventional female cruelty, Behn none the less gives ample indication of how capably she negotiated the inconvenience of being one of the so-called modest sex. Witness the defensive irony of 'To Alexis, On his saying, I loved a Man that talked much':

> Impertinence, my sexes shame,
> (Which has so long my life persued,)
> You with such modesty reclaim
> As all the woman has subdued,
> To so divine a power what must I owe,
> That renders me so like the perfect – you?
>> (ll.13-18)

By frequently couching her 'love' poems in a pastoral mould, Behn is enabled to write of real predicaments, as her biographers ably testify. And the reader senses that the fortunes of her thinly disguised shepherds and shepherdesses extend far beyond a delineation of Restoration Society. That Behn can so comfortably accommodate the world in which she lived to the pastoral tradition suggests how she saw the lineaments of sexual relationships (in a lamented, post-golden-age world) to be timeless and universal.

While Behn can be criticized for her limited range of vocabulary and some lack of discrimination in expression, the variety and quality of her achievement remains difficult to display adequately in an introduction to her poetry. A seminal work is her poem, 'The Golden Age', published in *Poems Upon Several Occasions* (1684). Here Behn evokes a pastoral innocence and freedom in order to expose the widest range of injustices and false virtues in contemporary society. The poem culminates in an attack upon the constraints of so-called 'honour': 'Nature's worse disease', as Behn neatly terms it, the pox by which women's natural inclinations are polluted. The fact that Behn alludes so often to the Golden Age discloses the tensions of a yearning in her poetry for broad harmonies which she knows can never be realized. Angeline Goreau speaks of the 'latent revolutionary implications in [Behn's] theory of man's original goodness', which she finds at odds with her loyalty to patriarchal Tory royalism. Janet Todd succinctly resolves the dilemma:

> As the invention of commerce traditionally marked the end of the golden age, so the growing influence of the city and newly labelled commercial Whigs marked the end of the modified restored golden age of the early Restoration. Throughout her life Behn railed against a mercantile ethos that reduced politics and sex to cash relations, making the crown an expensive ornament and the body a financial token.

She continues: 'she followed the Tory habit of equating Whigs with the regicide Puritans of the Interregnum, paralleling civil parliamentary upheavals of the 1680s with the Civil Wars of the 1640s.'[12]

Behn alludes to both these troubled periods when she denounces divinity in general, and the schism which it has prompted: 'the Gods / By teaching us religion first, first set the World at odds'. Her Golden Age is not just prelapsarian, but opposed to the prospect of the loss of Paradise specifically and severely established in patriarchal, Puritanical Old Testament teaching. The legacy of Eve's disobedience has been the debasement of womankind. By contrast, Behn's first women are conspicuously and blissfully unimplicated in the severities of Puritan Old Testament reprimand. 'Beneath [the] boughs the snakes securely dwelt', not invaded by any Satan:

> Not doing harm, nor harm from others felt;
> With whom the nymphs did innocently play,
> No spightful venom in the wantons lay;
> But to the touch were soft, and to the sight were gay.
>
> (III, 45-8)

Miltonic justifications of the ways of God to men (and women) are here and elsewhere repudiated in the writings of one female contemporary. Despite the wittiness of the correspondence between Behn's harmless snakes and the flaccid penis in the lines quoted,[13] the parallel points to the murky connections between man's lust and his 'spightful' appraisal of womankind. The erect and voluble serpent in Eden was the first rhetorically to ejaculate a 'spightful venom' which penetrated the ear of Mother Eve, and, in men's eyes, vilified the entirety of her otherwise desirable daughters in consequence. In her 'Paraphrase on the Lord's Prayer', published in the *Miscellany* of 1685, Behn clearly appreciates the true Christian legacy, and corrects the Old Testament bias of patriarchal practice.[14] Because the prayer Jesus Christ taught came from the mouth of one who gently reproved the woman taken in adultery,[15] under the rubric of 'Forgive us our Trespasses' Behn feels she can confess – and in a tone which suggests that little confession is needed – that 'Of all my crimes, the breach of all thy Laws / Love, soft bewitching Love! has been the cause'. Behn's serpentine 'charmer[s]' bedevil the situation by putting women in impossible situations. Two examples will suffice:

They fly if honour take our part,
Our virtue drives 'em o'er the field.
We lose 'em by too much desert,
And Oh! they fly us if we yield.
>   ('To Alexis in Answer to his Poem
>   against Fruition', ll.21-4)

Ah then how soon the amorous heat was laid!
How soon he broke the vows he made!
Slighting the trophies he had won.
And smiling saw me sigh for being undone.
>   ('Selinda and Cloris, made in an
>   Entertainment at Court', ll.35-8)

Eve is persuaded to inconstancy by the serpent. Behn's women, Behn's *personae*, are schooled in the vice by men. Their suffering might be good for poetry (nothing is more eloquent than Oenone's despair at desertion in the 'Paraphrase on Ovid's Epistle of Oenone to Paris'),[16] but scarcely veiled autobiographical reference frequently discloses a real hurt in Behn's verse, as in the controlled uncontrol of the following lines:

Make haste! make haste! my miserable soul,
To some unknown and solitary grove,
Where nothing may thy languishment control,
Where thou may'st never hear the name of love.
Where unconfined, and free, as whispering air
Thou may'st caress and welcome thy despair
>   ('On the first discovery of falseness in
>   Amintas', ll.1-6)

In recalling the self-sufficient fecundity of mother earth in 'The Golden Age', Behn comes close at one point to desiring the same for female kind, free from the violations of the opposite sex:

The stubborn plough had then,
Made no rude rapes upon the virgin Earth;
Who yielded of her own accord her plentious birth,
   Without the aids of men...
>   (III, 31-4)

If man after the Golden Age is portrayed as a desecrator, both sexes in the mythical past are seen as loving and faithful of their own accord. 'Uncontrolled' yet securely passionate before the Fall, male and female conduct has been blighted after it.

In emphasizing the status Behn once enjoyed, Janet Todd notes how she was judged to be among ' "the greatest Wits of the age" '.[17] 'Wit' is a notoriously difficult concept to pin down, especially in the seventeenth century when it gradually lost ground to notions of 'judgement'. But if we take it to involve surprising the reader with ingenious combinations of things otherwise thought to be dissimilar – in contrast with the neo-Classical Dr Johnson's strictures on 'heterogeneous ideas...yoked by violence together'[18] – then in Behn's poetry wit flourishes in her occasional addresses or eulogies, her elegies, and the baroque extravagances in which she complimented the House of Stuart. These odes catch the lyric measure and music of the English version of the grand Pindaric manner, which was initiated by Ben Jonson earlier in the century, and developed by Cowley and Behn's illustrious contemporary, John Dryden. Wit, considered as cleverness or stratagem, she reserves principally for her 'love' poems; especially perhaps for those addressed to women, which itself is a form of compliment to the intelligence of her own sex. 'To my Lady Morland at Tunbridge', for example, published in *Poems Upon Several Occasions*, concludes with generous and kindly advice which doubles as a very clever ruse to try to get her lover back from the younger beauty:

> But charming Cloris, you too meanly prize
> The more deserving glories of your eyes,
> If you permit him on an amorous score,
> To be your slave, who was my slave before.
> He oft has fetters worn, and can with ease
> Admit 'em or dismiss 'em when he please.
> A virgin-heart you merit, that ne'er found
> It could receive, till from your eyes, the wound;
> A heart that nothing but your force can fear,
> And own a soul as great as you are fair.
>
> (ll.41-50)[19]

xv

Lastly here, in our own serious times we should not overlook the fact that Behn is occasionally witty in the modern sense of the word. When she is in earnest it is never too long before the reader relishes an amusing or satiric anodyne.

As Behn's age gradually modified its metaphysical extravagances of expression with broader tones on the one hand, and more chastened forms of articulation on the other, so she proved mistress of the pithy couplet and the larger canvas. Whilst the attiring of the Queen in the lengthy *Pindaric Poem on the Happy Coronation of His Most Sacred Majesty James II* anticipates Belinda's robing in Pope's *The Rape of the Lock*, complete with the assistance of aerial sprites, so Behn's insistence that 'Wit is no more than nature well expressed' in her address *To Henry Higden, Esq; on his Translation of the Tenth Satire of Juvenal* predates by some twenty years that same poet's celebrated pronouncement on the subject among the brilliantly reasoned couplets of *An Essay on Criticism*. A judicious expansiveness appears in Behn's translations and paraphrases, and would seem to belie the fact that she was hampered by a woman's lack of formal education and had no Latin (or Greek). Or it indicates how well she managed either to translate from translation, or to write with the help of those male friends who had benefited from a proper training. Dryden's handsome compliment on her impressive 'Paraphrase on Oenone to Paris' is worth quoting here:

> the reader will here find most of the translations, with some little lattitude or variations from the authors sense: that of Oenone to Paris, is in Mr. Cowley's way of imitation only. I was desired to say that the author who is of the fair sex, understood not Latin. But if she does not, I am afraid she has given us occasion to be ashamed who do.[20]

In her poem 'To Mr. Creech (under the Name of Daphnis) on his Excellent Translation of Lucretius', Behn turns her deprivation into a gracious compliment to the addressee:

> thou has taught me more,
> Then all the mighty bards that went before.
> Others long since have palled the vast delight;

In duller Greek and Latin satisfied the appetite:
But I unlearned in schools disdain that mine
Should treated be at any feast but thine.

(ll.19-24)

Others (males) paradoxically have 'palled' their appetites for the Classics precisely because of their acquaintance with the languages in which they were written – 'duller' being an epithet flexible enough to apply to their whole laborious endeavour. Behn, by contrast, will serve her own 'appetite' to better effect through Creech's translation(s). Creech is placed in line with that 'Bard' whom Behn daringly positions as the civilized precursor of Godhead. One is inclined to think that the generosity of the compliment (once more an allusion to the sentiments of the Golden Age) and her own enthusiasm for enlightenment more than 'equals [Woman] to Man', and perhaps that was what Behn artfully meant to imply.

The struggle to sustain an equality of status was a hard one. No modern biographer of Behn has been able to resist lengthy quotation from the statement she made to accompany her play, *The Lucky Chance*, staged in 1686 and published the following year. 'All I ask, is the privilege for my masculine part the Poet in me ... to tread in those successful paths my predecessors have so long thrived in, to take those measures that both the Ancient and Modern writers have set me, and by which they have pleased the World so well.' Todd remarks that the 'conception of the "masculine part" owes something to the sense of gender fluidity in the early modern period when women were considered physically lesser than but not essentially different from men'.[21] In trying to fit Behn and her supplication into the vocabulary of established feminist theory, it would appear that she belongs in what Elaine Showalter has identified as the 'first ... prolonged phase of *imitation* of the prevailing modes of the dominant [male] tradition, and *internalization* of its standards of art and its views on social roles' – the *'feminine'*, rather than the later *'feminist'* and *'female'*, stage of women's writing.[22] Todd's observations on 'gender fluidity' are supported by the fact that no matter how much Behn desired to emulate her male predecessors, she sought equally the eternal glory of contemporary female peer and Classical sister. In a touching note interpolated into her translation of the sixth book of Cowley's *Of Plants*, 'the Translatress in her own Person speaks' of her desire to rest alongside Sappho, the ancient Greek lyricist, and 'the matchless Orinda', the poet and dramatist Katherine Philips (1631-64):

> ...after monarchs, poets claim a share
> As the next worthy thy prized wreaths to wear.
> Among that number, do not me disdain,
> Me, the most humble of thy glorious train.
> Let me with *Sappho* and *Orinda* be
> Oh ever sacred Nymph, adorned by thee:
> And give my verses immortality.

The body, however, was proving all-too transient. The Reverend Dr Gilbert Burnet, a figure of considerable importance and of markedly different persuasion from Mrs Behn in both temperament and politics, none the less kindly enquired after her health in her final days, and suggested that she might help relieve her distress by writing a poem in praise of the accession of William of Orange, Count of Nassau, and his consort Mary, daughter of her lamented James II. Behn, a woman of principle, declined, but did movingly argue her general sense of isolation and exclusion with a rare diplomatic grace and ability in the pindaric she addressed to Burnet himself. In her earlier 'Farewell to Celladon, On his Going into Ireland' she concedes the necessity of loyal service (in that case, to Charles II), although it be in conflict with her sense of loss at Celladon's departure. But in this later poem there is occasion for the kind of double-talk that Marvell exercised so cleverly in his 'Ode upon Cromwell's Return from Ireland'. Witness in the following lines, for example, cleverly dressed out as fulsome compliment, Behn's satiric disdain for Burnet's own partisan penmanship:

> Oh strange effect of a seraphic quill!
> That can by unperceptable degrees
> Change every notion, every principle
> To any form, its great dictator please:

The sword a feeble power, compared to that,
And to the nobler pen subordinate;
(v, 70-75)

What Behn did compose was her *Congratulatory Poem to her Sacred Majesty Queen Mary, Upon Her Arrival in England*. Behn's biographers have remarked on her Catholic connections and possible sympathies; and, when loyalty to the Catholic James's daughter compels her to swell the tribute, what is noticeable is the exercise of an adroit evasiveness whereby she stresses Mary's lineage at the expense of any reference to her unswervingly Protestant husband.

It is this poem and the pindaric to Burnet – the last work she herself saw through the press – which sadly and skilfully interweave Behn's private dilemmas with public events. She glances at the general mood of opportunism which accompanied the arrival of James's daughter and her Dutch prince – a mood in which, in a fine paradox, she finds her 'loyalty' cannot participate.

'I like the excluded Prophet stand,' she laments impressively, concluding: 'Your pen shall more immortalize his name, / Than even his own renowned and celebrated fame' ('Pindaric to Burnet'; see pp.95-8 below).

At the close of both life and works there remains the satiric sting in the tale: how cunningly her ironies expose the compromises of the great political divine, and how deftly that final couplet draws attention to the self-serving exaggerations of the panegyrist. Such clever turns in earnest, however, and so much more besides, are seemingly as nothing in the final analysis. Behn's tombstone bears the words: 'Here lies a proof that wit can never be / Defence enough against mortality'. The published works of other wits, principally male, at least give the illusion of bearing the lie to such laconic reflections. By the same means, Behn is beginning to enjoy, in O'Donnell's words, 'the Fame she deserves'.

Notes

[1] The compliments are taken from among the titles of poems dedicated to Aphra Behn on the publication of her *Poems Upon Several Occasions* (1684). See Montague Summers, ed., *The Works of Aphra Behn*, 6 vols. (New York: Phaeton Press, 1967), VI, 120-21, 124. (First published, 1915). George Woodcock called his helpful biography, *The Incomparable Aphra* (London: Boardman, 1948).

[2] At least where Behn the dramatist is concerned, some contemporary commentators have detected a clever, self-conscious strategy in her dealing with the role of 'female performer or writer'. See Bridget Orr, 'Whores' Rhetoric and the Maps of Love: constructing the Feminine in Restoration Erotica', in Clare Brant and Diane Purkiss, eds, *Women, Texts and Histories 1575-1760* (London: Routledge, 1992, 195-216. See also, generally, Jacqueline Pearson, *The Prostituted Muse: Images of Women and Women Dramatists 1642-1737* (New York/London: Harvester, 1988).

[3] Eric S. Robertson, *English Poetesses: a series of critical biographies with illustrative extracts* (London: 1883), 9.

[4] Mary Ann O'Donnell, *Aphra Behn: An Annotated Bibliography of Primary and Secondary Sources* (New York/London: Garland Publishing, Inc., 1986), 11.

[5] The brief outline which follows is principally indebted to Maureen Duffy's *The Passionate Shepherdess: Aphra Behn 1640-89* (London: Methuen, 1989), first published, 1977; to Jane Jones, 'New Light on the Background and Early Life of Aphra Behn', *Notes and Queries* (Sept, 1990), 288-93; and to the summaries, further suggestions, and cautionary admonishments in both O'Donnell's *Aphra Behn: An Annotated Bibliography*, Introduction, 1-11, and Volume I of Janet Todd's *The Works of Aphra Behn* (London: William Pickering, 1992), vii-xxxv, the first volume of a library edition in process of completion.

The most substantial disagreements in biographical tone and emphasis occur between Duffy and Angela Goreau. See the latter's *Reconstructing Aphra: A Social Biography of Aphra Behn* (O.U.P., 1980), in particular 296, fn 1. Goreau refers to Duffy's 1977 first edition. The second stands its ground with regard to both details and general approach. Subsequent commentators defer to Duffy, rather than Goreau.

[6] 'New Light on the Background and Early Life of Aphra Behn', 292.

[7] See *Aphra Behn: An Annotated Bibliography*, 1. Duffy reprints a selection of Behn's plays from Summers's text, without notes and with the briefest of introductions, in Aphra Behn, *Five Plays* (Methuen, 1990). *The Rover, Part I*, which she includes, has enjoyed a recent revival by the Royal Shakespeare Company. She is also responsible for the republication of Behn's novel, *Love-Letters between a Nobleman and his Sister* (London: Virago, 1987), based on a contemporary scandal. *Oroonoko* was published in an 'Everyman's Library' edition as early as 1930. See Philip Henderson, ed., *Shorter Novels: Seventeenth Century* (London: Dent). Janet Todd's library edition of Behn's *Works* should encourage broader and deeper critical thinking.

[8] Summers, *The Works of Aphra Behn*, I, xlvii.

[9] *Aphra Behn: An Annotated Bibliography*, 432.

[10]   Frederick M. Link, *Aphra Behn* (New York: Twayne Publishers Inc., 1968), 115.

[11]   A.C. Swinburne, *William Blake: A Critical Essay* (London, 1868), 131-2.

[12]   Todd, *The Works of Aphra Behn*, I, xxv. See Goreau, *Reconstructing Aphra*, 251-2. Kate Lilley briefly discusses Behn's golden age poetry in 'Blazing Worlds: Seventeenth century women's Utopian writing' in *Women, Texts and Histories 1575-1760*, 102-33.

[13]   Todd reminds us that 'the snake is frequently used as an image for the penis in seventeenth century poetry', *The Works of Aphra Behn*, I, 394 fn. An unfortunate modern pun has crept into the last line through the use of 'gay' for homosexual, (although it is thought that the most important man in Behn's romantic life, John Hoyle, caused her much anxiety because of his homosexual inclinations). Parallels between the snake and the phallus are clearly evident in Behn's poems, 'The Disappointment' (ll.101-10), and 'To the fair Clarinda, who made Love to Me, imagined more than woman' (ll.14-17).

[14]   Link crudely rejects this as the 'worst of her poems', *Aphra Behn*, 109.

[15]   See, in particular, *John* 8, vv.1-11.

[16]   This called forth generous praise from Dryden in his preface to the collection of *Ovid's Epistles, Translated by several Hands* (1680), where it was first published.

[17]   Todd, *The Works of Aphra Behn*, I, xliii.

[18]   Johnson's famous criticisms occur in his essay on Cowley in the *Lives of the Poets* (1779-81). Behn much admired Cowley (1618-67), translating (from a translation) a substantial part, Book VI, of his Latin *Platarum*, 'Of Plants'.

[19]   A shorter version of this poem appeared in *The Muses Mercury* (1707), under the title 'To Mrs Harsenet, on the Report of a Beauty, which she went to see at Church'. Harsenet was Lady Morland's maiden name, Mrs being a courtesy title. Goreau sees only generous spiritedness in the poem, while Duffy's 'sting at the end of [it]' is seen only in the compliment to Morland at the man's expense. See *Reconstructing Aphra*, 139-40; *The Passionate Shepherdess*, 116. Behn's 'Selinda and Cloris, made in an Entertainment at Court' (ll.5-15) makes the ruse to regain the lover abundantly clear: Selinda sees through Cloris's rehearsal of the advice which had appeared in 'To My Lady Morland at Tunbridge'.

[20]   See fn 16.

[21]   Todd, *The Works of Aphra Behn*, I, xxxv, fn 61.

[22]   Although Showalter's discussion occurs in her *A Literature of Their Own: British Women Novelists from Bronte to Lessing* (London: Virago Press, 1982, revised edn), in particular p.13, her by now well-assimilated comments appear to be of much broader literary and historical reference than the title of her book suggests. For modern reconsiderations of Behn's role in particular see, for example, fn 2.

Suggestions for Further Reading

Editions of Behn's Works:

Montague Summers, ed., *The Works of Aphra Behn*, 6 vols (New York: Phaeton Press, 1967), first published, 1915. Although incomplete, and with some questionable editorial decisions, the edition remains a useful one. Janet Todd (see below) praises the 'literary and anecdotal knowledge of the Restoration [Summers] reveals in his attributions and endnotes'.

Gerald Duchovnay, ed., 'Aphra Behn's *Oroonoko*: A Critical Edition' (Diss: Indiana University, 1971). A carefully edited edition, with a lengthy and valuable introduction.

Fidelis Morgan, ed., *The Female Wits: women playwrights on the London Stage* (London: Virago, 1981, 1989). Includes brief introduction to Behn and prints *The Lucky Chance*.

Maureen Duffy, ed., *Love-Letters between a Nobleman and his Sister* (London: Virago, 1987). Reprints Summers' text of Behn's novel, with an introduction.

Maureen Duffy, ed., *Five Plays* (Methuen, 1990). Reprints Summers' texts of *The Lucky Chance, The Rover, Part I, The Widow Ranter, The False Count*, and *Abdelazer*.

Janet Todd, ed., *The Works of Aphra Behn* (London: William Pickering, 1992-). A standard multi-volume library edition of Behn's works now in process of completion.

Bibliographies:

Mary Ann O'Donnell, *Aphra Behn: An Annotated Bibliography of Primary and Secondary Sources* (New York/London: Garland Publishing, Inc., 1986). An invaluable reference work, not least because it gives critical résumés of its exhaustive listings.

Secondary Sources:

George Woodcock, *The Incomparable Aphra* (London: Boardman, 1948). 'A sensible study' (O'Donnell), using contemporary documents to survey critical attitudes to Behn and her friendship with literary figures. Behn is seen as a 'revolutionary influence' working for women's rights, and as an important translator.

Frederick M. Link, *Aphra Behn* (New York: Twayne Publishers, Inc., 1968). A workmanlike appraisal of Behn and her work.

Angeline Goreau, *Reconstructing Aphra: A Social Biography of Aphra Behn* (O.U.P., 1980). An impassioned biography of Behn, the woman writer's life and work in the context of her times.

Jacqueline Pearson, *The Prostituted Muse: Images of Women and Women Dramatists 1642-1737* (New York/London: Harvester, 1988). Contains an extensive critique of the position and practice of women dramatists in the period specified, with a substantial chapter on the feminist Behn's playwriting career.

Maureen Duffy, *The Passionate Shepherdess: Aphra Behn 1640-89* (London: Methuen, 1989; first edition 1977). The most considered and thorough modern biography, setting Behn's life and work in its social, cultural, and political milieu.

Jane Jones, 'New Light on the Background and Early Life of Aphra Behn', *Notes and Queries* (Sept. 1990), 288-93. Restores the recently discredited assumption that Behn was the daughter of a barber, with new suggestions as to the identity of her husband.

Kate Lilley, 'Blazing Worlds: Seventeenth-Century Women's Utopian Writing', in Clare Brant and Diane Purkiss, eds, *Women, Texts and Histories 1575-1760* (London: Routledge, 1992), 102-33. Briefly discusses Behn's golden age attitudes.

Bridget Orr, 'Whores, Rhetoric and the Map of Love: constructing the Feminine in Restoration Erotica' in *Women, Texts and Histories 1575-1760*, 102-33. Contains revisionist remarks and notes on how Behn exploited her role(s) to advantage.

The Editions of Behn's Poetry

A large number of Behn's poems were first collected or published in her three miscellanies, the *Poems Upon Several Occasions* (1684), the *Miscellany* (1685), and the Miscellany appended to her *Lycidus: or the lover in fashion* (1688), with a few pieces appearing for the first time in the years following her death in 1689. Most of her substantial occasional poems were first published separately in the 1680s. Volume VI of Montague Summers' pioneering but imperfect edition of *The Works of Aphra Behn* (1915, reprinted 1967) includes the poetry but omits the occasional poems on state affairs. Volume I of Janet Todd's *The Works of Aphra Behn* (1992) gives the poetry entire. Her multi-volume library edition of Behn's writings is now in process of completion.

There are problems for establishing copy texts. For example, Mary Ann O'Donnell, in the introduction to *Aphra Behn: An Annotated Bibliography*, states that 'if a poem was published more than once... the later states [of the texts Behn supervised] should be considered more authoritative' (p.9); while Janet Todd observes that 'many of Behn's poems appear in at least two forms, and it is not a matter of the last version's being the definitive one, but of versions being created for different purposes and circumstances' (*Works*, I, xxxvii). For full discussion of the complexities of publishing history and practice, the reader is referred to O'Donnell generally; and, in particular, to the extended considerations which Todd offers in her edition of the poetry: *Works*, I, xxxvi-liii.

The present selection is based on Montague Summers' edition of the miscellanies and other works (with corrections of occasional printing errors) in comparison with copies of the earlier editions. These latter form the basis for the selections from the poems on state occasions.

The Restoration period was particularly extravagant in its choices of typeface, with which the subsequent editions of Behn have been obliged to reach a compromise. In this selection the poems have for the first time been modernized. What can be argued as the arbitrary, or excessive, employment of italics and capital letters has been removed; and spelling (particularly where contractions are concerned) has been made to conform to current practice except where an alteration might affect metre or pronunciation.

The Golden Age

A Paraphrase on a Translation out of French

I

Blest Age! when ev'ry purling stream
    Ran undisturbed and clear,
When no scorned shepherds on your banks were seen,
Tortured by love, by jealousy, or fear;
When an eternal Spring dressed ev'ry bough,
And blossoms fell, by new ones dispossessed;
These their kind shade affording all below,
And those a bed where all below might rest.
The groves appeared all dressed with wreaths of flowers,
And from their leaves dropped aromatic showers,   10
Whose fragrant heads in mystic twines above,
Exchanged their sweets, and mixed with thousand kisses,
    As if the willing branches strove
    To beautify and shade the grove
    Where the young wanton gods of love
Offer their noblest sacrifice of blisses.

II

Calm was the air, no winds blew fierce and loud,
The sky was darkened with no sullen cloud;
But all the heav'ns laughed with continued light,
And scattered round their rays serenely bright.   20
    No other murmurs filled the ear
    But what the streams and rivers purled,
When silver waves o'er shining pebbles curled;
  Or when young zephyrs fanned the gentle breeze,
  Gath'ring fresh sweets from balmy flowers and trees,
Then bore 'em on their wings to perfume all the air:
    While to their soft and tender play,
    The gray-plumed natives of the shades
Unwearied sing till love invades,   [30
Then bill, then sing again while love and music makes the day.

1

III

The stubborn plough had then,
Made no rude rapes upon the virgin Earth;
Who yielded of her own accord her plentious birth,
    Without the aids of men;
  As if within her teeming womb,
  All nature, and all sexes lay,
  Whence new creations every day
  Into the happy world did come:
  The roses filled with morning Dew,
    Bent down their loaded heads,   40
T'adorn the careless shepherds grassy beds
While still young opening buds each moment grew
And as those withered, dressed his shaded couch anew;
Beneath whose boughs the snakes securely dwelt,
Not doing harm, nor harm from others felt;
With whom the nymphs did innocently play,
No spightful venom in the wantons lay;
But to the touch were soft, and to the sight were gay.

IV

Then no rough sounds of wars alarms,
Had taught the world the needless use of arms: 50
    Monarchs were uncreated then,
Those arbitrary rulers over men:
Kings that made laws, first broke 'em, and the gods
By teaching us religion first, first set the world at odds:
    Till then ambition was not known,
That poison to content, bane to repose;
Each swain was lord o'er his own will alone,
His innocence religion was, and laws.
Nor needed any troublesome defence
    Against his neighbours insolence.   60
Flocks, herds, and every necessary good
Which bounteous nature had designed for food,
Whose kind increase o'er-spread the meads and plains,
Was then a common sacrifice to all th'agreeing swains.

2

V

Right and property were words since made,
  When power taught mankind to invade:
When pride and avarice became a trade;
   Carried on by discord, noise and wars,
   For which they bartered wounds and scars;
And to enhance the merchandise, miscalled it, Fame,   70
   And rapes, invasions, tyrannies,
   Was gaining of a glorious name:
Stiling their savage slaughters, victories;
   Honour, the error and the cheat
   Of the ill-natured busy great,
   Nonsense, invented by the proud,
   Fond idol of the slavish crowd,
   Thou wert not known in those blest days
Thy poison was not mixed with our unbounded joys;
Then it was glory to pursue delight,   80
And that was lawful all, that pleasure did invite,
Then 'twas the amorous world enjoyed its reign;
And tyrant Honour strove t' usurp in vain.

VI

The flowry Meads, the rivers and the groves,
Were filled with little gay-winged loves:
  That ever smiled and danced and played,
And now the woods, and now the streams invade,
And where they came all things were gay and glad:
When in the myrtle groves the lovers sat
Oppressed with a too fervent heat;   90
A thousand cupids fanned their wings aloft,
And through the boughs the yielded air would waft:
Whose parting leaves discovered all below,
And every god his own soft power admired,
And smiled and fanned and sometimes bent his bow;
Where e'er he saw a shepherd uninspired.
The nymphs were free, no nice, no coy disdain;
Denied their joys, or gave the lover pain;

3

The yielding maid but kind resistance makes;
Trembling and blushing are not marks of shame,   100
   But the effect of kindling flame:
Which from the sighing burning swain she takes,
While she with tears all soft, and down-cast-eyes,
Permits the charming conqueror to win the prize.

VII

The lovers thus, thus uncontrolled did meet,
Thus all their joys and vows of love repeat:
     Joys which were everlasting, ever new
     And every vow inviolably true:
Not kept in fear of gods, no fond religious cause,
Nor in obedience to the duller laws.   110
Those fopperies of the gown were then not known,
Those vain, those politic curbs to keep man in,
Who by a fond mistake created that a sin;
Which freeborn we, by right of nature claim our own.
   Who but the learned and dull moral fool
Could gravely have forseen, man ought to live by rule?

VIII

Oh cursed Honour! thou who first didst damn,
  A woman to the sin of shame;
    Honour! that robb'st us of our gust,
    Honour! that hindered mankind first,   120
At loves eternal spring to quench his amorous thirst.
Honour! who first taught lovely eyes the art,
  To wound, and not to cure the heart:
With love to invite, but to forbid with awe,
And to themselves prescribe a cruel law;
    To veil 'em from the lookers on,
    When they are sure the slave's undone,
And all the charming'st part of beauty hid;
Soft looks, consenting wishes, all denied.
    It gathers up the flowing hair,   130

That loosely played with wanton air.
The envious net, and stinted order hold,
The lovely curls of jet and shining gold;
No more neglected on the shoulders hurled:
Now dressed to tempt, not gratify the world:
Thou, miser Honour, hord'st the sacred store,
And starv'st thy self to keep thy votaries poor.

IX

Honour! that putt'st our words that should be free
    Into a set formality.
Thou base debaucher of the generous heart,   140
That teachest all our looks and actions art;
    What love designed a sacred gift,
    What nature made to be possessed;
    Mistaken Honour, made a theft,
    For glorious love should be confessed:
For when confined, all the poor lover gains,
Is broken sighs, pale looks, complaints and pains.
Thou foe to pleasure, nature's worst disease,
    Thou tyrant over mighty kings,
What mak'st thou here in shepherds cottages;   150
Why troublest thou the quiet shades and springs?
    Be gone, and make thy famed resort
       To princes palaces;
Go deal and chaffer in the trading court,
That busy market for fantastic things;
Be gone and interrupt the short retreat,
    Of the illustrious and the great;
    Go break the politicians sleep,
    Disturb the gay ambitious fool,
    That longs for sceptres, crowns, and rule,   160
Which not his title, nor his wit can keep;
But let the humble honest swain go on,
In the blest paths of the first rate of man;
    That nearest were to gods allied,
And formed for love alone, disdained all other pride.

X

Be gone! and let the golden age again,
　　　Assume its glorious reign;
　　Let the young wishing maid confess,
　　What all your arts would keep concealed:
　　The mystery will be revealed,　　　　　　　　　170
And she in vain denies, whilst we can guess,
She only shows the jilt to teach man how,
To turn the false artillery on the cunning foe.
　　Thou empty vision hence, be gone,
　　　And let the peaceful swain love on;
The swift paced hours of life soon steal away:
　　Stint not, ye gods, his short lived joy.
The Spring decays, but when the Winter's gone,
　　The trees and flowers anew comes on;
The Sun may set, but when the night is fled,　　　180
　　And gloomy darkness does retire,
　　He rises from his watry bed:
All glorious, gay, all dressed in amorous fire.
　　But Sylvia when your beauties fade,
When the fresh roses on your cheeks shall die,
　　Like flowers that wither in the shade,
Eternally they will forgotten lie,
And no kind Spring their sweetness will supply.
When snow shall on those lovely tresses lie.
And your fair eyes no more shall give us pain,　　190
　　But shoot their pointless darts in vain.
What will your duller honour signify?
Go boast it then! and see what numerous store
Of lovers will your ruined shrine adore.
　　Then let us, Sylvia, yet be wise,
　　And the gay hasty minutes prize:
The Sun and Spring receive but our short light,
Once set, a sleep brings an eternal night.

On a Juniper Tree, cut down to make Busks

Whilst happy I triumphant stood,
The pride and glory of the wood;
My aromatic boughs and fruit,
Did with all other trees dispute.
Had right by nature to excel,
In pleasing both the taste and smell:
But to the touch I must confess,
Bore an ungrateful sullenness.
My wealth, like bashful virgins, I
Yielded with some reluctancy;   10
For which my value should be more,
Not giving easily my store.
My verdant branches all the year
Did an eternal beauty wear;
Did ever young and gay appear.
Nor needed any tribute pay,
For bounties from the God of day:
Nor do I hold supremacy,
(In all the wood) o'er every tree.
But even those too of my own race,   20
That grow not in this happy place.
But that in which I glory most,
And do myself with reason boast,
Beneath my shade the other day,
Young Philocles and Cloris lay,
Upon my root she leaned her head,
And where I grew, he made their bed:
Whilst I the canopy more largely spread.
Their trembling limbs did gently press,
The kind supporting yielding grass: 30
Ne'er half so blest as now, to bear
A swain so young, a nymph so fair:
My grateful shade I kindly lent,
And every aiding bough I bent.
So low, as sometimes had the bliss,
To rob the shepherd of a kiss,

Whilst he in pleasures far above
The sense of that degree of love:
Permitted every stealth I made,
Unjealous of his rival shade.   40
I saw 'em kindle to desire,
Whilst with soft sighs they blew the fire;
Saw the approaches of their joy,
He growing more fierce, and she less coy,
Saw how they mingled melting rays,
Exchanging love a thousand ways.
Kind was the force on every side,   ⎫
Her new desire she could not hide: ⎬
Nor would the shepherd be denied.   ⎭
Impatient he waits no consent   50
But what she gave by languishment,
The blessed minute he pursued,
Whilst love her fear and shame subdued;
And now transported in his arms,
Yields to the conqueror all her charms,
His panting breast, to hers now joined,
They feast on raptures unconfined;
Vast and luxuriant, such as prove
The immortality of love.
For who but a divinity,   ⎫   60
Could mingle Souls to that degree; ⎬
And melt 'em into extasy?   ⎭
Now like the Phoenix both expire,   ⎫
While from the ashes of their fire, ⎬
Sprung up a new, and soft desire.   ⎭
Like charmers, thrice they did invoke,
The God! and thrice new vigour took.
Nor had the mystery ended there,
But Cloris reassumed her fear,
And chid the swain, for having pressed,   70
What she alas would not resist:
Whilst he in whom loves sacred flame,
Before and after was the same,
Fondly implored she would forget

A fault, which he would yet repeat.
From active joys with some they haste,
To a reflexion on the past;
A thousand times my covert bless,
That did secure their happiness:
Their gratitude to every tree   80
They pay, but most to happy me;
The shepherdess my bark caressed,
Whilst he my root, love's pillow, kissed;
And did with sighs, their fate deplore,
Since I must shelter them no more;
And if before my joys were such,
In having heard, and seen too much,
My grief must be as great and high,
When all abandoned I shall be,   90
Doomed to a silent destiny.
No more the charming strife to hear,
The shepherds vows, the virgins fear:
No more a joyful looker on,
Whilst loves soft battle's lost and won.
  With grief I bowed my murmuring head,
And all my crystal dew I shed.
Which did in Cloris pity move,
(Cloris whose soul is made of love;)
She cut me down, and did translate,
My being to a happier state.   100
No martyr for religion died
With half that unconsidering pride;
My top was on that altar laid,
Where Love his softest offerings paid:
And was as fragrant incense burned,
My body into busks was turned:
Where I still guard the sacred store,
And of Loves temple keep the door.

On the Death of Mr Grinhil, the Famous Painter

I

What doleful cries are these that fright my sense,
Sad as the groans of dying Innocence?
The killing accents now more near approach,
    And the infectious sound,
  Spreads and enlarges all around;
And does all hearts with grief and wonder touch.
  The famous Grinhil dead! even he,
That could to us give immortality;
  Is to the eternal silent groves withdrawn,
Those sullen groves of everlasting dawn;   10
Youthful as flowers, scarce blown, whose opening leaves,
A wond'rous and a fragrant prospect gives,
Of what its elder beauties would display,
When they should flourish up to rip'ning May.
Witty as Poets, warmed with love and wine,
  Yet still spared heaven and his friend,
For both to him were sacred and divine:
Nor could he this no more than that offend.
Fixt as a martyr where he friendship paid,
    And generous as a god,   20
Distributing his bounties all abroad;
And soft and gentle as a love-sick maid.

II

Great master of the noblest mystery,
That ever happy knowledge did inspire;
  Sacred as that of poetry,
And which the wond'ring world does equally admire.
  Great Natures work we do condemn,
When on his glorious births we meditate:
The face and eyes, more darts received from him,
  Then all the charms she can create.   30
The difference is, his beauties do beget
In the enamoured soul a virtuous heat:

While Natures grosser pieces move,
In the coarse road of common love:
So bold, yet soft, his touches were;
So round each part's, so sweet and fair.
That as his pencil moved men thought it pressed,
The lively imitating rising breast,
Which yield like clouds, where little angels rest:
The limbs all easy as his temper was;   40
Strong as his mind, and manly too;
Large as his soul his fancy was, and new:
And from himself he copied every grace,
For he had all that could adorn a face,
All that could either sex subdue.

III

Each excellence he had that youth has in its pride,
And all experienced age could teach,
At once the vigorous fire of this,
And every virtue which that could express.
In all the heights that both could reach;   50
And yet alas, in this perfection died.
Dropped like a blossom with the Northern blast,
(When all the scattered leaves abroad were cast;)
As quick as if his fate had been in haste:
So have I seen an unfixed star,
Out-shine the rest of all the numerous train,
As bright as that which guides the mariner,
Dart swiftly from its darkened sphere:
And ne'er shall sight the world again.

IV

Ah why should so much knowledge die!   60
Or with his last kind breath,
Why could he not to some one friend bequeath
The mighty legacy!
But 'twas a knowledge given to him alone,

11

That his eternized name might be
  Admired to all posterity,
By all to whom his grateful name was known.
  Come all ye softer beauties, come;
  Bring wreaths of flowers to deck his tomb;
Mixed with the dismal cypress and the yew,   70
  For he still gave your charms their due:
And from the injuries of age and time,
  Preserved the sweetness of your prime:
And best knew how t' adore that sweetness too;
  Bring all your mournful tributes here,
And let your eyes a silent sorrow wear,
Till every virgin for a while become
Sad as his fate, and like his picture's dumb.

A Ballad on Mr. J.H. to Amoret, asking why I was so sad

  My Amoret, since you must know,
  The grief you say my eyes do show:
  Survey my heart, where you shall find,
  More love than for yourself confined.
  And though you chide, you'll pity too,
  A passion which even rivals you.

  Amyntas on a holiday
  As fine as any lord of May,
  Amongst the nymphs, and jolly swains,
  That feed their flocks upon the plains: 10
  Met in a grove beneath whose shade,
  A match of dancing they had made.

  His cassock was of green, as trim
  As grass upon a river brim;
  Untouched or sullied with a spot,
  Unpressed by either lamb or goat:

12

And with the air it loosely played,
With every motion that he made.

His sleeves a-many ribbons ties,
Where one might read love-mysteries: 20
As if that way he would impart,
To all, the sentiments of his heart,
Whose passions by those colours known,
He with a charming pride would own.

His bonnet with the same was tied,
A silver scrip hung by his side:
His buskins garnished a-la-mode,
Were graced by every step he trod;
Like Pan, a majesty he took,
And like Apollo when he spoke.   30

His hook a wreath of flowers braid,
The present of some love-sick maid,
Who all the morning had bestowed,
And to her fancy now composed:
Which fresher seemed when near that place,
To whom the giver captive was.

His eyes their best attracts put on,
Designing some should be undone;
For he could at his pleasure move,
The nymphs he liked to fall in love: 40
Yet so he ordered every glance,
That still they seemed but wounds of chance.

He well could feign an innocence,
And taught his silence eloquence;
Each smile he used, had got the force,
To conquer more than soft discourse:
Which when it served his ends he'd use,
And subtly through a heart infuse.

His wit was such it could control
The resolutions of a soul;   50
That a religious vow had made,
By love it ne'er would be betrayed:
For when he spoke he well could prove
Their errors who dispute with love.

With all these charms he did address
Himself to every shepherdess:
Until the bag-pipes which did play,
Began the bus'ness of the day;
And in the taking forth to dance,
The lovely swain became my chance.   60

To whom much passion he did vow,
And much his eyes and sighs did show;
And both employed with so much art,
I strove in vain to guard my heart;
And ere the night our revels crost,
I was entirely won and lost.

Let me advise thee, Amoret,
Fly from the baits that he has set
In every grace; which will betray
All beauties that but look that way:
But thou hast charms that will secure   70
A captive in this conquerour.

Song

Love Armed

Love in fantastic triumph sat,
Whilst bleeding hearts around him flowed,
For whom fresh pains he did create,
And strange tyrannic power he showed;

From thy bright eyes he took his fire,
Which round about, in sport he hurled;
But 'twas from mine he took desire,
Enough to undo the amorous world.

From me he took his sighs and tears,
From thee his pride and cruelty;
From me his languishments and fears,
And every killing dart from thee;
Thus thou and I, the God have armed,
And set him up a deity;
But my poor heart alone is harmed,
Whilst thine the victor is, and free.

To Mr. Creech (under the Name of Daphnis) on his Excellent Translation of Lucretius

Thou great young man! Permit amongst the crowd
Of those that sing thy mighty praises loud,
My humble Muse to bring its tribute too.
  Inspired by thy vast flight of verse,
Methinks I should some wondrous thing rehearse,
Worthy divine Lucretius, and diviner thou.
    But I of feebler seeds designed,
    Whilst the slow moving atoms strove,
    With careless heed to form my mind:
    Composed it all of softer love.   10
  In gentle numbers all my songs are dressed,
    And when I would thy glories sing,
  What in strong manly verse I would express,
Turns all to womanish tenderness within,
Whilst that which admiration does inspire,
In other souls, kindles in mine a fire.
Let them admire thee on – whilst I this newer way
    Pay thee yet more than they:

15

For more I owe, since thou hast taught me more,
Then all the mighty bards that went before. 20
Others long since have palled the vast delight;
In duller Greek and Latin satisfied the appetite:
But I unlearned in schools, disdain that mine
Should treated be at any feast but thine.
Till now, I cursed my birth, my education,
And more the scanted customs of the nation:
Permitting not the female sex to tread,
The mighty paths of learned heroes dead.
The god-like Virgil, and great Homers verse,
Like divine mysteries are concealed from us. 30
    We are forbid all grateful themes,
     No ravishing thoughts approach our ear,
    The fulsome gingle of the times,
Is all we are allowed to understand or hear.
  But as of old, when men unthinking lay,
Ere gods were worshipped or ere laws were framed
The wiser Bard that taught 'em first t' obey,
Was next to what he taught, adored and famed;
Gentler they grew, their words and manners changed,
And savage now no more the woods they ranged. 40
So thou by this translation dost advance
Our knowledge from the state of ignorance,
And equals us to Man! Ah how can we,
Enough adore, or sacrifice enough to thee.

The mystic terms of rough Philosophy,
Thou dost so plain and easily express;
Yet deck'st them in so soft and gay a dress:
So intelligent to each capacity,
That they at once instruct and charm the sense,
With heights of fancy, heights of eloquence; 50
And reason over all unfettered plays,
Wanton and undisturbed as summers breeze;
  That gliding murmurs o'er the trees:
And no hard notion meets or stops its way.
  It pierces, conquers and compels,

Beyond poor feeble faith's dull oracles.
    Faith the despairing souls content,
Faith the last shift of routed argument.

Hail sacred Wadham! whom the Muses grace,
And from the rest of all the reverend pile   60
Of noble palaces, designed thy space:
    Where they in soft retreat might dwell.
They blest thy fabric, and said – do thou,
        Our darling sons contain;
We thee our sacred nursery ordain,
        They said and blest, and it was so.
And if of old the fanes of sylvan gods,
    Were worshipped as divine abodes;
        If courts are held as sacred things,
            For being the awful seats of kings: 70
        What veneration should be paid,
To thee that hast such wondrous poets made?
To gods for fear, devotion was designed,
And safety made us bow to majesty;
Poets by nature awe and charm the mind,
Are born not made by dull religion or necessity.

The learned Thirsis did to thee belong,
Who Athens plague has so divinely sung.
Thirsis to wit, as sacred friendship true,
Paid mighty Cowley's memory its due.   80
Thirsis who whilst a greater plague did reign,
Than that which Athens did depopulate:
Scattering rebellious fury o'er the plain,
That threatened ruin to the Church and State,
Unmoved he stood, and feared no threats of fate.
That loyal champion for the Church and Crown,
That noble ornament of the sacred gown,
Still did his Sovereign's cause espouse,
And was above the thanks of the mad senate-house.
Strephon the Great, whom last you sent abroad,   90
Who writ, and loved, and looked like any god;

For whom the Muses mourn, the love-sick maids
Are languishing in melancholy shades.
  The Cupids flag their wings, their bows untie,
  And useless quivers hang neglected by,
  And scattered arrows all around 'em lie.
By murmuring brooks the careless deities are laid,
Weeping their rifled power now noble Strephon's dead.

Ah sacred Wadham! should'st thou never own
But this delight of all mankind and thine;   100
For ages past of dulness, this alone,
  This charming hero would atone.
And make thee glorious to succeeding time;
But thou like Natures self disdain'st to be,
  Stinted to singularity.
Even as fast as she thou dost produce,
And over all the sacred mystery infuse.
No sooner was famed Strephon's glory set,
Strephon the soft, the lovely and the great;
But Daphnis rises like the morning-star,   110
That guides the wandring traveller from afar.
Daphnis whom every Grace, and Muse inspires,
Scarce Strephons ravishing poetic fires
So kindly warm, or so divinely cheer.

Advance young Daphnis, as thou hast begun,
  So let thy mighty race be run.
  Thou in thy large poetic chase,
  Begin'st where others end the race.
If now thy grateful numbers are so strong,
If they so early can such graces show,   120
Like beauty so surprising, when so young,
What Daphnis will thy riper judgment do,
When thy unbounded verse in their own streams shall flow!
  What wonder will they not produce,   ⎫
  When thy immortal fancy's loose;   ⎬
Unfettered unconfined by any other muse!   ⎭
Advance young Daphnis then, and mayst thou prove

Still sacred in thy poetry and love.
May all the groves with Daphnis songs be blessed,
Whilst every bark is with thy disticks dressed.   130
May timorous maids learn how to love from thence
And the glad shepherd arts of eloquence.
And when to solitude thou would'st retreat,
May their tuned pipes thy welcome celebrate.
And all the nymphs strow garlands at thy feet.
May all the purling streams that murmuring pass,
    The shady groves and banks of flowers,
    The kind reposing beds of grass,
    Contribute to their softer hours.
Mayst thou thy Muse and mistress there caress,   140
And may one heighten t'others happiness.
And whilst thou so divinely dost converse,
We are content to know and to admire thee in thy sacred verse.

To Mrs. W. On her Excellent Verses (Writ in Praise of some I had made on the Earl of Rochester) Written in a Fit of Sickness

Enough kind Heaven! to purpose I have lived,
And all my sighs and languishments survived.
My stars in vain their sullen influence have shed,
    Round my till now unlucky head:
I pardon all the silent hours I've grieved,
My weary nights, and melancholy days;
    When no kind power my pain relieved,
I lose you all, ye sad remembrancers,
    I lose you all in new-born joys,
Joys that will dissipate my falling tears.   10
The mighty soul of Rochester's revived,
Enough kind Heaven to purpose I have lived.
I saw the lovely phantom, no disguise,
Veiled the blest vision from my eyes,

19

'Twas all o'er Rochester that pleased and did surprise.
Sad as the grave I sat by glimmering light,
Such as attends departing souls by night.
Pensive as absent lovers left alone,
Or my poor dove, when his fond mate was gone.
Silent as groves when only whispering gales,   20
    Sigh through the rushing leaves,
As softly as a bashful shepherd breaths,
    To his loved nymph his amorous tales.
So dull I was, scarce thought a subject found,
Dull as the light that gloomed around;
    When lo the mighty spirit appeared,
    All gay, all charming to my sight;
    My drooping soul it raised and cheered,
    And cast about a dazzling light.
    In every part there did appear,   30
    The great, the god-like Rochester,
His softness all, his sweetness everywhere.
It did advance, and with a generous look,
To me addressed, to worthless me it spoke:
With the same wonted grace my Muse it praised,
With the same goodness did my faults correct;
And careful of the fame himself first raised,
Obligingly it schooled my loose neglect.
The soft, the moving accents soon I knew
The gentle voice made up of harmony;   40
Through the known paths of my glad soul it flew;
I knew it straight, it could no others be,
'Twas not allied but very very he.
    So the all-ravished swain that hears
    The wondrous Music of the Spheres,
For ever does the grateful sound retain,
    Whilst all his oaten pipes and reeds,
The rural music of the groves and meads,
Strive to divert him from the heavenly song in vain.
    He hates their harsh and untuned lays,   50
Which now no more his soul and fancy raise.
But if one note of the remembered air

He chance again to hear,
He starts, and in a transport cries, – *'Tis there.*
He knows it all by that one little taste,
And by that grateful hint remembers all the rest.
Great, good, and excellent, by what new way
Shall I my humble tribute pay,
For this vast glory you my Muse have done,
For this great condescension shown! 60
So gods of old sometimes laid by
Their awful trains of majesty,
And changed ev'n Heav'n awhile for groves and plains,
And to their fellow-gods preferred the lowly swains,
And beds of flowers would oft compare
To those of downy clouds, or yielding air;
At purling streams would drink in homely shells,
Put off the God, to revel it in woods and shepherds cells;
Would listen to their rustic songs, and show
Such divine goodness in commending too, 70
Whilst the transported swain the honour pays
With humble adoration, humble praise.

The Return

Amyntas, whilst you
Have an art to subdue,
And can conquer a heart with a look or a smile;
You pitiless grow,
And no faith will allow;
'Tis the glory you seek when you rifle the spoil.

Your soft warring eyes,
When prepared for the prize,
Can laugh at the aids of my feeble disdain;
You can humble the foe,
And soon make her to know
Though she arms her with pride, her efforts are but vain.

But shepherd beware,
Though a victor you are;
A tyrant was never secure in his throne;
Whilst proudly you aim
New conquests to gain,
Some hard-hearted nymph may return you your own.

On a Copy of Verses made in a Dream, and sent to me in a Morning before I was Awake

Amyntas, if your wit in dreams
Can furnish you with themes,
What must it do when your soul looks abroad,
Quick'nd with agitations of the sense,
And dispossessed of sleeps dull heavy load,
When ev'ry syllable has eloquence?
And if by chance such wounds you make,
And in your sleep such welcome mischiefs do;
What are your powers when you're awake,
Directed by design and reason too?   10

I slept, as duller mortals use,
Without the music of a thought,
When by a gentle breath, soft as thy Muse,
Thy name to my glad ear was brought:
Amyntas! cried the page – and at the sound,
My list'ning soul unusual pleasure found.
So the harmonious Spheres surprise,
Whilst the all-ravished shepherd gazes round,
And wonders whence the charms should rise,
That can at once both please and wound.   20
Whilst trembling I unripped the seal
Of what you'd sent,
My heart with an impatient zeal,
Without my eyes, would needs reveal
Its bus'ness and intent.

But so beyond the sense they were
Of ev'ry scribbling lovers common art,
    That now I find an equal share
Of love and admiration in my heart.
    And while I read, in vain I strove   30
        To hide the pleasure which I took;
    Bellario saw in ev'ry look
    My smiling joy and blushing love.
Soft ev'ry word, easy each line, and true;
    Brisk, witty, manly, strong and gay;
    The thoughts are tender all, and new,
And fancy ev'rywhere does gently play,
        Amyntas, if you thus go on,
Like an unwearied conqueror day and night,
    The world at last must be undone.   40
    You do not only kill at sight,
    But like a Parthian in your flight,
    Whether you rally or retreat,
    You still have arrows for defeat.

To my Lady Morland at Tunbridge

As when a conqu'ror does in triumph come,
And proudly leads the vanquished captives home,
The joyful people crowd in ev'ry street,
And with loud shouts of praise the victor greet;
While some whom chance or fortune kept away,
Desire at least the story of the day;
How brave the Prince, how gay the chariot was,
How beautiful he looked with what a grace;
Whether upon his head he plumes did wear;
Or if a wreath of bays adorned his hair: 10
They hear 'tis wondrous fine, and long much more
To see the Hero than they did before.
So when the marvels by report I knew,

Of how much beauty, Cloris, dwelt in you;
How many slaves your conqu'ring eyes had won,
And how the gazing crowd admiring throng:
I wished to see, and much a lover grew
Of so much beauty, though my rivals too.
I came and saw, and blest my destiny;
I found it just you should out-rival me.   20
'Twas at the altar, where more hearts were giv'n
To you that day, then were addressed to Heav'n.
The rev'rend man whose age and mystery
Had rendered youth and beauty vanity,
By fatal chance casting his eyes your way,
Mistook the duller bus'ness of the day,
Forgot the Gospel, and began to pray.
Whilst the enamoured crowd that near you pressed
Receiving darts which none could e'er resist,
Neglected the mistake o'th' love-sick priest.   30
Ev'n my devotion, Cloris, you betrayed,
And I to Heaven no other petition made,
But that you might all other nymphs out-do
In cruelty as well as beauty too.
I called Amyntas faithless Swain before,
But now I find 'tis just he should adore.
Not to love you, a wonder sure would be,
Greater than all his perjuries to me.
And whilst I blame him, I excuse him too;
Who would not venture Heav'n to purchase you?   40
But charming Cloris, you too meanly prize
The more deserving glories of your eyes,
If you permit him on an amorous score,
To be your slave, who was my slave before.
He oft has fetters worn, and can with ease
Admit 'em or dismiss 'em when he please.
A virgin-heart you merit, that ne'er found
It could receive, till from your eyes, the wound;
A heart that nothing but your force can fear,
And own a soul as great as you are fair.   50

24

The Disappointment

One day the amorous Lysander,
By an impatient passion swayed,
Surprised fair Cloris, that loved maid,
Who could defend her self no longer.
All things did with his love conspire;
The gilded planet of the day,
In his gay chariot drawn by fire,
Was now descending to the sea,
And left no light to guide the world,
But what from Cloris brighter eyes was hurled.   10

In a lone thicket made for love,
Silent as yielding maids consent,
She with a charming languishment,
Permits his force, yet gently strove;
Her hands his bosom softly meet,
But not to put him back designed,
Rather to draw 'em on inclined:
Whilst he lay trembling at her feet,
Resistance 'tis in vain to show;
She wants the power to say – *Ah! What d'ye do?*   20

Her bright eyes sweet, and yet severe,
Where love and shame confus'dly strive,
Fresh vigour to Lysander give;
And breathing faintly in his ear,
She cried – *Cease, cease – your vain desire,*
Or I'll call out – What would you do?
My dearer honour ev'n to you
I cannot, must not give – Retire,
Or take this life, whose chiefest part
I gave you with the conquest of my heart.   30

But he as much unused to fear,
As he was capable of love,
The blessed minutes to improve,

25

Kisses her mouth, her neck, her hair;
Each touch her new desire alarms,
His burning trembling hand he pressed
Upon her swelling snowy breast,
While she lay panting in his arms.
All her unguarded beauties lie
The spoils and trophies of the enemy.   40

And now without respect or fear,
He seeks the object of his vows,
(His love no modesty allows)
By swift degrees advancing – where
His daring hand that altar seized,
Where gods of love do sacrifice:
That awful throne, that paradise
Where rage is calmed and anger pleased;
That fountain where delight still flows,
And gives the universal world repose.   50

Her balmy lips encount'ring his,
Their bodies, as their souls, are joined;
Where both in transports unconfined
Extend themselves upon the moss.
Cloris half dead and breathless lay;
Her soft eyes cast a humid light,
Such as divides the day and night;
Or falling stars, whose fires decay:
And now no signs of life she shows,
But what in short-breathed sighs returns and goes.   60

He saw how at her length she lay;
He saw her rising bosom bare;
Her loose thin robes, through which appear
A shape designed for love and play;
Abandoned by her pride and shame.
She does her softest joys dispense,
Off'ring her virgin-innocence
A victim to loves sacred flame;

While the o'er-ravished shepherd lies
Unable to perform the sacrifice.   70

Ready to taste a thousand joys,
The too transported hapless swain
Found the vast pleasure turned to pain;
Pleasure which too much love destroys:
The willing garments by he laid,
And heaven all opened to his view,
Mad to possess, himself he threw
On the defenceless lovely maid.
But Oh what envying god conspires
To snatch his power, yet leave him the desire!   80

Nature's support, (without whose aid
She can no human being give)
Itself now wants the art to live;
Faintness its slackened nerves invade:
In vain th' enraged youth essayed
To call its fleeting vigour back,
No motion 'twill from motion take;
Excess of love his love betrayed:
In vain he toils, in vain commands;
The Insensible fell weeping in his hand.   90

In this so amorous cruel strife,
Where love and fate were too severe,
The poor Lysander in despair
Renounced his reason with his life:
Now all the brisk and active fire
That should the nobler part inflame,
Served to increase his rage and shame,
And left no spark for new desire:
Not all her naked charms could move
Or calm that rage that had debauched his love.   100

Cloris returning from the trance
Which love and soft desire had bred,

Her timorous hand she gently laid
(Or guided by design or chance)
Upon that fabulous Priapus,
That potent god, as poets feign;
But never did young shepherdess,
Gath'ring of fern upon the plain,
More nimbly draw her fingers back,
Finding beneath the verdant leaves a snake: 110

Than Cloris her fair hand withdrew,
Finding that god of her desires
Disarmed of all his awful fires,
And cold as flow'rs bathed in the morning dew.
Who can the Nymph's confusion guess?
The blood forsook the hinder place,
And strewed with blushes all her face,
Which both disdain and shame expressed:
And from Lysander's arms she fled,
Leaving him fainting on the gloomy bed.   120

Like lightning through the grove she hies,
Or Daphne from the Delphic God,
No print upon the grassy road
She leaves, t' instruct pursuing eyes.
The wind that wantoned in her hair,
And with her ruffled garments played,
Discovered in the flying maid
All that the gods e'er made, if fair.
So Venus, when her Love was slain,
With fear and haste flew o'er the fatal plain.   130

The Nymph's resentments none but I
Can well imagine or condole:
But none can guess Lysander's soul,
But those who swayed his destiny.
His silent griefs swell up to storms,
And not one god his fury spares;
He cursed his birth, his fate, his stars;

But more the shepherdess's charms,
Whose soft bewitching influence
Had damned him to the Hell of impotence.   140

On a Locket of Hair Wove in a True-Loves Knot, given me by Sir R.O.

What means this knot, in mystic order tied,
And which no human knowledge can divide?
Not the great conqu'rors sword can this undo
Whose very beauty would divert the blow.
  Bright relic! Shrouded in a shrine of gold!
Less myst'ry made a deity of old.
Fair charmer! Tell me by what powerful spell
You into this confused order fell?
If magic could be wrought on things divine,
Some amorous sybil did thy form design   10
In some soft hour, which the prophetic maid
In nobler mysteries of love employed.
Wrought thee a hieroglyphic, to express
The wanton God in all his tenderness;
Thus shaded, and thus all adorned with charms,
Harmless, unfletched, without offensive arms,
He used of old in shady groves to play,
Ere swains broke vows, or nymphs were vain and coy,   }
Or Love himself had wings to fly away.
  Or was it (his almighty power to prove)   20
Designed a quiver for the God of Love?
And all these shining hairs which th'inspired maid
Has with such strange mysterious fancy laid,
Are meant his shafts; the subtlest surest darts
That ever conquered or secured his hearts;
Darts that such tender passions do convey,
Not the young wounder is more soft than they.
  'Tis so; the riddle I at last have learned:
But found it when I was too far concerned.

A letter to a Brother of the Pen in Tribulation

Poor Damon! Art thou caught? Is't even so?
Art thou become a *tabernacler too?
Where sure thou dost not mean to preach or pray,
Unless it be the clean contrary way:
This holy time[a] I little thought thy sin
Deserved a tub to do its penance in.
O how you'll for th' Egyptian flesh-pots wish,
When you're half-famished with your Lenten-dish,
Your almonds, currants, biscuits hard and dry,
Food that will soul and body mortify: 10
Damned penitential drink, that will infuse
Dull principles into thy grateful Muse.
– Pox on't that you must needs be fooling now,
Just when the Wits had greatest need[b] of you.
Was Summer then so long a coming on,
That you must make an artificial one?
Much good may't do thee; but 'tis thought thy brain
Ere long will wish for cooler days again.
For honesty no more will I engage:
I durst have sworn thou'dst had thy pusillage.   20
Thy looks the whole cabal have cheated too;
But thou wilt say, most of the Wits do so.
Is this thy writing[c] plays? who thought thy wit
An interlude of whoring would admit?
To poetry no more thou'lt be inclined,
Unless in verse to damn all woman-kind:
And 'tis but just thou shouldst in rancour grow
Against that sex that has confined thee so.
    All things in nature now are brisk and gay
At the approaches of the blooming May: 30
The new-fletched birds do in our arbours sing
A thousand airs to welcome in the Spring;
Whilst ev'ry swain is like a bridegroom dressed,

* So he called a sweating-tub.
(a) Lent.   (b) I wanted a prologue to a play.   (c) He pretended to retire to write.

And ev'ry nymph as going to a feast:
The meadows now their flowry garments wear,
And ev'ry grove does in its bride appear:
Whilst thou poor Damon in close rooms are pent,
Where hardly thy own breath can find a vent.
Yet that too is a heaven, compared to th' task
Of coddling every morning in a cask.   40
   Now I could curse this female, but I know,
She needs it not, that thus could handle you.
Besides, that vengeance does to thee belong.
And 'twere injustice to disarm thy tongue.
Curse then, dear swain, that all the youth may hear,
And from thy dire mishap be taught to fear.
Curse till thou hast undone the race, and all
That did contribute to thy Spring and Fall.

The Reflection: A Song

Poor lost Serena, to bemoan
   The rigour of her fate,
Highed to a river-side alone,
   Upon whose brinks she sat.
Her eyes, as if they would have spared,
   The language of her tongue,
In silent tears a while declared
   The sense of all her wrong.

But they alas too feeble were,
   Her grief was swoln too high   10
To be expressed in sighs and tears;
   She must or speak or die.
And thus at last she did complain,
   Is this the faith, said she,
Which thou allowest me, cruel swain,
   For that I gave to thee?

Heaven knows with how much innocence
   I did my soul incline
To thy soft charms of eloquence,
   And gave thee what was mine. 20
I had not one reserve in store,
   But at thy feet I laid
Those arms that conquered heretofore,
   Though now thy trophies made.

Thy eyes in silence told their tale
   Of love in such a way,
That 'twas as easy to prevail,
   As after to betray.
And when you spoke my list'ning soul,
   Was on the flattery hung: 30
And I was lost without control,
   Such music graced thy tongue.

Alas how long in vain you strove
   My coldness to divert!
How long besieged it round with love,
   Before you won the heart.
What arts you used, what presents made,
   What songs, what letters writ:
And left no charm that could invade,
   Or with your eyes or wit. 40

Till by such obligations pressed,
   By such dear perjuries won:
I heedlessly resigned the rest,
   And quickly was undone.
For as my kindling flames increase,
   Yours glimmeringly decay:
The rifled joys no more can please,
   That once obliged your stay.

Witness ye springs, ye meads and groves,
   Who oft were conscious made 50

To all our hours and vows of love;
  Witness how I'm betrayed.
Trees drop your leaves, be gay no more,
  Ye rivers waste and dry:
Whilst on your melancholy shore,
  I lay me down and die.

Song

Ah! what can mean that eager joy
Transports my heart when you appear?
Ah, Strephon! you my thoughts employ
In all that's charming, all that's dear.
When you your pleasing story tell,
A softness does invade each part,
And I with blushes own I feel
Something too tender at my heart.

At your approach my blushes rise,
And I at once both wish and fear;
My wounded soul mounts to my eyes,
As it would prattle stories there.
Take, take that heart that needs must go;
But, shepherd, see it kindly used:
For who such presents will bestow,
If this, alas! should be abused?

To Lysander, who made some Verses on a
Discourse of Loves Fire

In vain, dear youth, you say you love,
And yet my marks of passion blame:
Since jealousy alone can prove,
The surest witness of my flame:
And she who without that, a love can vow,
Believe me, shepherd, does not merit you.

Then give me leave to doubt, that fire
I kindle, may another warm:
A face that cannot move desire,
May serve at least to end the charm: 10
Love else were witchcraft, that on malice bent,
Denies ye joys, or makes ye impotent.

'Tis true, when cities are on fire,
Men never wait for crystal springs;
But to the neighb'ring pools retire;
Which nearest, best assistance brings;
And serves as well to quench the raging flame,
As if from god-delighting streams it came.

A fancy strong may do the feat
Yet this to love a riddle is,   20
And shows that passion but a cheat;
Which men but with their tongues confess.
For 'tis a maxim in loves learned school,
Who blows the fire, the flame can only rule.

Though honour does your wish deny,
Honour! the foe to your repose;
Yet 'tis more noble far to die,
Than break loves known and sacred laws:
What lover would pursue a single game,
That could amongst the fair deal out his flame?   30

Since then, Lysander, you desire,
Amynta only to adore;
Take in no partners to your fire,
For who well loves, that loves one more?
And if such rivals in your heart I find,
Tis in my power to die, but not be kind.

A Dialogue for an Entertainment at Court, between Damon and Sylvia

Damon

Ah, Sylvia! if I still pursue,
Whilst you in vain your scorn improve;
What wonders might your eyes not do:
If they would dress themselves in love.

Silvia

Shepherd, you urge my love in vain,
For I can ne'er reward your pain;
A slave each smile of mine can win,
    And all my soft'ning darts,
Whene'er I please, can bring me in
A thousand yielding hearts.   10

Damon

Yet if those slaves you treat with cruelty,
    'Tis an inglorious victory;
And those unhappy swains you so subdue,
May learn at last to scorn, as well as you;
    Your beauty though the gods designed
    Should be adored by all below;
Yet if you want a godlike pitying mind,
Our adoration soon will colder grow:
    'Tis pity makes a deity,
    Ah, Silvia! deign to pity me,   20
And I will worship none but thee.

Sylvia

Perhaps I may your counsel take,
And pity though not love, for Damons sake;
  Love is a flame my heart ne'er knew,
Nor knows how to begin to burn for you.

Damon

Ah, Sylvia, who's the happy swain,
For whom that glory you ordain!
Has Strephon, Pithius, Hilus, more
Of youth, of love, or flocks a greater store?
My flame pursues you too, with that address,   30
  Which they want passion to profess:
Ah then make some returns my charming shepherdess.

Silvia

Too faithful shepherd, I will try my heart,
And if I can will give you part.

Damon

Oh that was like your self expressed,
Give me but part, and I will steal the rest.

Silvia

Take care, young swain, you treat it well,
If you would have it in your bosom dwell;
Now let us to the shades retreat,
Where all the nymphs and shepherds meet.   40

Damon

And give me there your leave my pride to show,
For having but the hopes of conquering you;
Where all the swains shall passion learn of me:
  And all the nymphs to bless like thee.

Silvia

Where every grace I will bestow,
And every look and smile, shall show
How much above the rest I value you.

Damon

And I those blessings will improve;
By constant faith, and tender love.

[A Chorus of Satyrs and Nymphs
made by another hand.]

To Lysander, on some Verses he writ, and asking more for his Heart then 'twas worth

Take back that heart, you with such caution give,
   Take the fond valued trifle back;
I hate love-merchants that a trade would drive;
   And meanly cunning bargains make.

I care not how the busy market goes,
   And scorn to chaffer for a price:
Love does one staple rate on all impose,
   Nor leaves it to the traders choice.

A heart requires a heart unfeigned and true,
   Though subtly you advance the price,   10
And ask a rate that simple love ne'er knew:
   And the free trade monopolise.

An humble slave the buyer must become,
   She must not bate a look or glance,
You will have all, or you'll have none;
   See how loves market you enhance.

Is't not enough, I gave you heart for heart,
   But I must add my lips and eyes;
I must no friendly smile or kiss impart;
   But you must dun me with advice.   20

And every hour still more unjust you grow,
   Those freedoms you my life deny,
You to Adraste are obliged to show,
   And give her all my rifled joy.

Without control she gazes on that face,
   And all the happy envied night,
In the pleased circle of your fond embrace:
   She takes away the lovers right.

From me she ravishes those silent hours,
   That are by sacred love my due;   30
Whilst I in vain accuse the angry Powers,
   That make me hopeless love pursue.

Adrastes ears with that dear voice are blessed,
   That charms my soul at every sound,
And with those love-enchanting touches pressed:
   Which I ne'er felt without a wound.

She has thee all: whilst I with silent grief,
   The fragments of thy softness feel,
Yet dare not blame the happy licensed thief:
   That does my dear-bought pleasures steal.   40

Whilst like a glimmering taper still I burn,
   And waste my self in my own flame,
Adraste takes the welcome rich return:
   And leaves me all the hopeless pain.

Be just, my lovely swain, and do not take
   Freedoms you'll not to me allow;
Or give Amynta so much freedom back:
   That she may rove as well as you.

Let us then love upon the honest square,
   Since interest neither have designed,   50
For the sly gamester, who ne'er plays me fair,
   Must trick for trick expect to find.

To the Honourable Edward Howard, on his Comedy called The New Utopia

I

Beyond the merit of the age,
You have adorned the stage;
So from rude farce, to comic order brought,
    Each action, and each thought;
To so sublime a method, as yet none
    (But mighty Ben alone)
Could e'er arive, and he at distance too;
Were he alive he must resign to you:
    You have out-done whate'er he writ,
In this last great example of your wit.   10
Your Solymour does his Morose destroy,
And your Black Page undoes his Barbers Boy;
All his collegiate ladies must retire,
While we thy braver heroines do admire.
    This new Utopia raised by thee
Shall stand a structure to be wondered at,
And men shall cry, this – this – is he
Who that poetic city did create:
Of which More only did the model draw,
You did complete that little world, and gave it law.   20

II

If you too great a prospect do allow
To those whom ignorance does at distance seat,
'Tis not to say, the object is less great,
But they want sight to apprehend it so:
    The ancient poets in their times,
When through the peopled streets they sung their rhymes,
Found small applause; they sung but still were poor;
Repeated wit enough at every door
T'have made 'em demigods! but 'twould not do,
Till ages more refined esteemed 'em so.   30
The modern poets have with like success,

Quitted the stage, and sallied from the press.
    Great Jonson scarce a play brought forth,
But monster-like it frighted at its birth:
    Yet he continued still to write,
And still his satire did more sharply bite.
    He writ though certain of his doom,
    Knowing his power in comedy:
    To please a wiser age to come:
And though he weapons wore to justify   40
The reasons of his pen; he could not bring,
Dull souls to sense by satire, nor by cudgelling.

III

    In vain the errors of the times
You strive by wholesome precepts to confute.
    Not all your power in prose or rhymes
        Can finish the dispute
'Twixt those that damn, and those that do admire
The heat of your poetic fire.
    Your soul of thought you may employ
        A nobler way,   50
Than in revenge upon a multitude,
    Whose ignorance only makes 'em rude.
        Should you that justice do,
    You must for ever bid adieu,
        To poetry divine,
        And ev'ry Muse o'th' nine:
For Malice then with Ignorance would join,
    And so undo the world and you:
    So ravish from us that delight
    Of seeing the wonders which you write: 60
And all your glories unadmired must lie,
    As vestal beauties are entombed before they die.

Consider and consult your wit,
Despise those ills you must endure:
And raise your scorn as great as it,
Be confident and then secure.
   And let your rich-fraught pen
   Adventure out again;
Maugre the storms that do opose its course,
Storms that destroy without remorse: 70
    It may new worlds decry,
   Which peopled from thy brain may know
More than the Universe besides can show:
More arts of love, and more of gallantry.
Write on! and let not after ages say,
The whistle or rude hiss could lay
   Thy mighty spright of Poetry,
   Which but the fools and guilty fly;
   Who dare not in thy mirror see
    Their own deformity: 80
Where thou in two, the world dost character,
Since most of men Sir Graves, or Peacocks are.

And shall that Muse that did erewhile,
Chant forth the glories of the British isle,
   Shall she who louder was than fame;
    Now useless lie, and tame?
She who late made the Amazons so great,
   And she who conquered Scythia too;
   (Which Alexander ne'er could do)
   Will you permit her to retreat?   90
   Silence will like submission show:
   And give advantage to the foe!
Undaunted let her once again appear,
And let her loudly sing in every ear:
Then like thy mistress' eyes, who have the skill,

Both to preserve and kill;
So thou at once may'st be revenged on those
That are thy foes,
And on thy friends such obligations lay,
As nothing but the deed the doer can repay.   100

To Lysander at the Music-Meeting

It was too much, ye Gods, to see and hear;
Receiving wounds both from the eye and ear:
One charm might have secured a victory,
Both, raised the pleasure even to ecstasy:
So ravished lovers in each others arms,
Faint with excess of joy, excess of charms:
Had I but gazed and fed my greedy eyes,
Perhaps you'd pleased no farther than surprise.
That heav'nly form might admiration move,
But, not without the music, charmed with love: 10
At least so quick the conquest had not been;
You stormed without, and harmony within:
Nor could I listen to the sound alone,
But I alas must look – and was undone:
I saw the softness that composed your face,
While your attention heightened every grace:
Your mouth all full of sweetness and content,
And your fine killing eyes of languishment:
Your bosom now and then a sigh would move,
(For music has the same effects with love.)   20
Your body easy and all tempting lay,
Inspiring wishes which the eyes betray,   }
In all that have the fate to glance that way:
A careless and a lovely negligence,
Did a new charm to every limb dispense:
So look young angels, listening to the sound,
When the tuned Spheres glad all the Heav'ns around:
So raptured lie amidst the wondering crowd,

42

So charmingly extended on a cloud.
　　When from so many ways loves arrows storm,　　} 　　30
Who can the heedless heart defend from harm?
Beauty and music must the soul disarm;
Since harmony, like fire to wax, does fit
The softened heart impressions to admit:
As the brisk sounds of war the courage move,
Music prepares and warms the soul to love.
But when the kindling sparks such fuel meet,
No wonder if the flame inspired be great.

An Ode to Love

Dull Love no more thy senseless arrows prize,
Damn thy gay quiver, break thy bow;
　　'Tis only young Lysanders eyes,
　　That all the arts of wounding know.

A pox of foolish politics in love,
A wise delay in war the foe may harm:
By lazy siege while you to conquest move;
His fiercer beauties vanquish by a storm.

Some wounded god, to be revenged on thee,
The charming youth formed in a lucky hour,　　　　10
Dressed him in all that fond divinity,
That has out-rivalled thee, a god, in power.

　　Or else while thou supinely laid
　　Basking beneath some myrtle shade,
　　In careless sleep, or tired with play,
　　When all thy shafts did scattered lie;
　　Th'unguarded spoils he bore away,
And armed himself with the artillery.

The sweetness from thy eyes he took,
The charming dimples from thy mouth,　　　　　　20

That wonderous softness when you spoke;
And all thy everlasting youth.

Thy bow, thy quiver, and thy darts:
Even of thy painted wing has rifled thee,
To bear him from his conquered broken hearts,
  To the next fair and yielding she.

A Paraphrase on Ovid's Epistle of Œnone to Paris

THE ARGUMENT.

Hecuba, being with child of Paris, dreamed she was delivered of a firebrand: Priam, consulting the Prophets, was answered the child should be the destruction of Troy, wherefore Priam commanded it should be delivered to wild beasts as soon as born; but Hecuba conveys it secretly to Mount Ida, there to be fostered by the shepherds, where he falls in love with the nymph Œnone, but at last being known and owned, he sails into Greece, and carries Helen to Troy, which Œnone understanding, writes him this epistle.

To thee, dear Paris, lord of my desires,
Once tender partner of my softest fires;
To thee I write, mine, while a shepherd's swain,
But now a prince, that title you disdain.
Oh fatal romp, that could so soon divide
What love, and all our sacred vows had tied!
What god, our love industrious to prevent,
Curst thee with power, and ruined my content?
Greatness, which does at best but ill agree
With love, such distance sets 'twixt thee and me.   10
Whilst thou a prince, and I a shepherdess,
My raging passion can have no redress.
Would God, when first I saw thee, thou hadst been
This great, this cruel, celebrated thing.
That without hope I might have gazed and bowed,
And mixed my adorations with the crowd;

Unwounded then I had escaped those eyes,
Those lovely authors of my miseries.
Not that less charms their fatal power had dressed,
But fear and awe my love had then suppressed: 20
My unambitious heart no flame had known,
But what devotion pays to gods alone.
I might have wondered and have wished that he,
Whom heaven should make me love, might look like thee.
More in a silly nymph had been a sin,
This had the height of my presumption been.
But thou a flock didst feed on Ida's plain,
And hadst no title, but the lovely swain.
A title! which more virgin hearts has won,
Than that of being owned King Priam's son.   30
Whilst me a harmless neighbouring cottager
You saw, and did above the rest prefer.
You saw! and at first sight you loved me too,
Nor could I hide the wounds received from you.
Me all the village herdsmen strove to gain,   ⎫
For me the shepherds sighed and sued in vain,   ⎬
Thou hadst my heart, and they my cold disdain.   ⎭
Not all their offerings, garlands, and first born
Of their loved ewes, could bribe my native scorn.
My love, like hidden treasure long concealed,   40
Could only where 'twas destined, be revealed.
And yet how long my maiden blushes strove
Not to betray my easy new-born love.
But at thy sight the kindling fire would rise,
And I, unskilled, declare it at my eyes.
But oh the joy! the mighty ecstasy
Possessed thy soul at this discovery.
Speechless, and panting at my feet you lay,
And short breathed sighs told what you could not say.
A thousand times my hand with kisses pressed,   50
And looked such darts, as none could e'er resist.
Silent we gazed, and as my eyes met thine,
New joy filled theirs, new love and shame filled mine!
You saw the fears my kind disorder showed

And breaking silence faith anew you vowed!
Heavens, how you swore by every power divine
You would be ever true! be ever mine!
Each god, a sacred witness you invoke,
And wished their curse whene'er these vows you broke.
Quick to my heart each perjured accent ran,   60
Which I took in, believed, and was undone.
    Vows are love's poisoned arrows, and the heart
So wounded, rarely finds a cure from art.
At least this heart which fate has destined yours, ⎱
This heart unpractised in love's mystic powers, ⎬
For I am soft and young as April flowers.   ⎰
    Now uncontrolled we meet, unchecked improve
Each happier minute in new joys of love!
Soft were our hours! and lavishly the day
We gave entirely up to love, and play.   70
Oft to the cooling groves our flocks we led, ⎱
And seated on some shaded, flowery bed,   ⎬
Watched the united wantons as they fed.   ⎰
And all the day my list'ning soul I hung   ⎱
Upon the charming music of thy tongue,   ⎬
And never thought the blessed hours too long. ⎰
No swain, no god like thee could ever move,   ⎱
Or had so soft an art in whisp'ring love.   ⎬
No wonder for thou art allied to Jove!   ⎰
And when you piped, or sung, or danced, or spoke,   80
The God appeared in every grace, and look.
Pride of the swains, and glory of the shades,
The grief, and joy of all the love-sick maids.
Thus whilst all hearts you ruled without control,
I reigned the absolute Monarch of your soul.
    Each beech my name yet bears, carved out by thee,
Paris, and his Œnone fill each tree;
And as they grow, the letters larger spread,
Grow still a witness of my wrongs when dead!
    Close by a silent silver brook there grows ⎱   90
A poplar, under whose dear gloomy boughs   ⎬
A thousand times we have exchanged our vows!   ⎰

Oh may'st thou grow! t' an endless date of years!
Who on thy bark this fatal record bears;
When Paris *to* Œnone *proves untrue,*
Back Xanthus *streams shall to their fountains flow.*
Turn! turn your tides! back to your fountains run!
The perjured swain from all his faith is gone!
  Cursed be that day, may fate appoint the hour,
As ominous in his black calendar;   100
When Venus, Pallas, and the Wife of Jove
Descended to thee in the myrtle grove,
In shining chariots drawn by winged clouds:
Naked they came, no veil their beauty shrouds;
But every charm, and grace exposed to view,
Left heav'n to be surveyed, and judged by you.
To bribe thy voice Juno would crowns bestow,
Pallas more gratefully would dress thy brow
With wreaths of wit! Venus proposed the choice
Of all the fairest Greeks! and had thy voice.   110
Crowns, and more glorious wreaths thou didst despise,
And promised beauty more than empire prize!
This when you told, Gods! what a killing fear ⎫
Did over all my shivering limbs appear?   ⎬
And I presaged some ominous change was near! ⎭
The blushes left my cheeks, from every part
The blood ran swift to guard my fainting heart.
You in my eyes the glimmering light perceived ⎫
Of parting life, and on my pale lips breathed   ⎬
Such vows, as all my terrors undeceived.   ⎭   120
But soon the envying gods disturbed our joy,
Declared thee great! and all my bliss destroy!
  And now the fleet is anchored in the bay,
That must to Troy the glorious youth convey.
Heavens! how you looked! and what a godlike grace
At their first homage beautified your face!
Yet this no wonder, or amazement brought,
You still a monarch were in soul, and thought!
Nor could I tell which most the news augments,
Your joys of power, or parting discontents.   130

You kissed the tears which down my cheeks did glide,
And mingled yours with the soft falling tide,
And 'twixt your sighs a thousand times you said,
Cease, my Œnone! Cease, my charming maid!
If Paris lives his native Troy to see,
My lovely nymph, thou shalt a princess be!
But my prophetic fears no faith allowed,
My breaking heart resisted all you vowed.
Ah must we part, I cried! that killing word
No farther language could to grief afford.   140
Trembling, I fell upon thy panting breast,
Which was with equal love, and grief oppressed   ⎫
Whilst sighs and looks, all dying spoke the rest.   ⎭
About thy neck my feeble arms I cast,
Not vines, nor ivy circle elms so fast.
To stay, what dear excuses didst thou frame,
And fanciedst tempests when the seas were calm?
How oft the winds contrary feigned to be,
When they, alas, were only so to me!
How oft new vows of lasting faith you swore,   150
And 'twixt your kisses all the old run o'er?
    But now the wisely grave, who love despise,
(Themselves past hope) do busily advise.
Whisper renown, and glory in thy ear,
Language which lovers fright, and swains ne'er hear.
For Troy, they cry! these shepherds weeds lay down,
Change crooks for sceptres! garlands for a crown!
But sure that crown does far less easy sit,
Than wreaths of flowers, less innocent and sweet.
Nor can thy beds of state so grateful be,   160
As those of moss, and new fall'n leaves with me!
    Now tow'rds the beach we go, and all the way
The groves, the fern, dark woods, and springs survey;
That were so often conscious to the rites
Of sacred love, in our dear stoln delights.
With eyes all languishing, each place you view,
And sighing cry, *Adieu, dear shades, adieu!*
Then 'twas thy soul e'en doubted which to do,

Refuse a crown, or those dear shades forego!
Glory and Love! the great dispute pursued,   170
But the false Idol soon the God subdued.
  And now on board you go, and all the sails
Are loosened to receive the flying gales.
Whilst I, half dead on the forsaken strand,   ⎫
Beheld thee sighing on the deck to stand,   ⎬
Wafting a thousand kisses from thy hand.   ⎭
And whilst I could the lessening vessel see,
I gazed, and sent a thousand sighs to thee!
And all the sea-born Nereids implore
Quick to return thee to our rustic shore.   180
  Now like a ghost I glide through ev'ry grove,   ⎫
Silent, and sad as death, about I rove,   ⎬
And visit all our treasuries of love!   ⎭
This shade th'account of thousand joys does hide,
As many more this murmuring rivers side,
Where the dear grass, still sacred, does retain
The print, where thee and I so oft have lain.
Upon this oak thy pipe, and garland's placed,
That sycamore is with thy sheep-hook graced.
Here feed thy flock, once loved though now thy scorn,   190
Like me forsaken, and like me forlorn!
  A rock there is, from whence I could survey   ⎫
From far the bluish shore, and distant sea,   ⎬
Whose hanging top with toil I climbed each day,   ⎭
With greedy view the prospect I ran o'er,
To see what wished for ships approached our shore.
One day all hopeless on its point I stood,
And saw a vessel bounding o'er the flood,
And as it nearer drew, I could discern
Rich purple sails, silk cords, and golden stern;   200
Upon the deck a canopy was spread   ⎫
Of antique work in gold and silver made,   ⎬
Which mixed with sun-beams dazzling light displayed. ⎭
But oh! beneath this glorious scene of state
(Cursed be the sight) a fatal beauty sat.
And fondly you were on her bosom laid,

49

Whilst with your perjured lips her fingers played;
Wantonly curled and dallied with that hair,
Of which, as sacred charms, I bracelets wear.
   Oh! hadst thou seen me then in that mad state,   210
So ruined, so designed for death and fate,
Fixed on a rock, whose horrid precipice
In hollow murmurs wars with angry seas;
Whilst the bleak winds aloft my garments bear,
Ruffling my careless and dishevelled hair,
I looked like the sad statue of Despair.
With out-stretched voice I cried, and all around
The rocks and hills my dire complaints resound.
I rent my garments, tore my flattering face,
Whose false deluding charms my ruin was.   220
Mad as the seas in storms, I breathe despair,
Or winds let loose in unresisting air.
Raging and frantic through the woods I fly,
And Paris! lovely, faithless Paris cry.
But when the echos sound thy name again,
I change to new variety of pain.
For that dear name such tenderness inspires,
And turns all passion to loves softer fires:
With tears I fall to kind complaints again,
So tempests are allayed by showers of rain.   230
   Say, lovely youth, why wouldst thou thus betray
My easy faith, and lead my heart astray?
I might some humble shepherd's choice have been,
Had I that tongue ne'er heard, those eyes ne'er seen.
And in some homely cot, in low repose,
Lived undisturbed with broken vows and oaths:
All day by shaded springs my flocks have kept,
And in some honest arms at night have slept.
Then unupbraided with my wrongs thou'dst been
Safe in the joys of the fair Grecian Queen: 240
What stars do rule the great? no sooner you
Became a prince, but you were perjured too.
Are crowns and falsehoods then consistent things?
And must they all be faithless who are kings?

The Gods be praised that I was humbly born,
Even though it renders me my Paris scorn.
For I had rather this way wretched prove,
Than be a queen and faithless in my love.
Not my fair rival would I wish to be,
To come prophaned by others joys to thee.   250
A spotless maid into thy arms I brought,
Untouched in fame, ev'n innocent in thought;
Whilst she with love has treated many a guest,
And brings thee but the leavings of a feast:
With Theseus from her country made escape,
Whilst she miscalled the willing flight, a rape.
So now from Atreus son, with thee is fled,
And still the rape hides the adult'rous deed.
And is it thus great ladies keep entire
That virtue they so boast, and you admire?   260
Is this a trick of courts, can ravishment
Serve for a poor evasion of consent?
Hard shift to save that honour prized so high,
Whilst the mean fraud's the greater infamy.
How much more happy are we rural maids,
Who know no other palaces than shades?
Who wish no title to enslave the crowd,
Lest they should babble all our crimes aloud;
No arts our good to show, our ill to hide,
Nor know to cover faults of love with pride.   270
I loved, and all love's dictates did pursue,
And never thought it could be sin with you.
To gods, and men, I did my love proclaim;
For one soft hour with thee, my charming swain,
Would recompence an age to come of shame,
Could it as well but satisfy my fame.
But oh! those tender hours are fled and lost,
And I no more of fame, or thee can boast!
Twas thou wert honour, glory, all to me:
Till swains had learned the vice of perjury,   280
No yielding maids were charged with infamy.
'Tis false and broken vows make love a sin,

Hadst thou been true, we innocent had been.
But thou less faith than Autumn leaves do'st show,
Which ev'ry blast bears from their native bough.
Less weight, less constancy, in thee is born,
Than in the slender mildewed ears of corn.
Oft when you garlands wove to deck my hair, ⎫
Where mystic pinks, and daisies mingled were, ⎬
You swore 'twas fitter diadems to bear: ⎭
And when with eager kisses pressed my hand,
Have said, *How well a Sceptre 'twould command!*
And when I danced upon the flow'ry green, ⎫
With charming, wishing eyes survey my mien, ⎬
And cry! the Gods designed thee for a queen! ⎭
Why then for Helen dost thou me forsake?
Can a poor empty name such difference make?
Besides if love can be a sin, thine's one,
To Menelaus Helen does belong.
Be just, restore her back, she's none of thine,
And, charming Paris, thou art only mine.
'Tis no ambitious flame that makes me sue
To be again beloved, and blessed by you;
No vain desire of being allied t' a king, ⎫
Love is the only dowry I can bring, ⎬
And tender love is all I ask again; ⎭
Whilst on her dang'rous smiles fierce war must wait
With fire and vengeance at your palace gate,
Rouse your soft slumbers with their rough alarms,
And rudely snatch you from her faithless arms:
Turn then, fair fugitive, ere 'tis too late,
Ere thy mistaken love procures thy fate;
Ere a wronged husband does thy death design,
And pierce that dear, that faithless heart of thine.

290

300

310

Song

Cease, cease, Aminta, to complain,
    Thy languishment give o'er,
Why shoud'st thou sigh because the swain
    Another does adore?
Those charms, fond maid, that vanquished thee,
    Have many a conquest won,
And sure he could not cruel be,
    And leave 'em all undone.

The youth a noble temper bears,
    Soft and compassionate,   10
And thou canst only blame thy stars,
    That made thee love too late;
Yet had their influence all been kind
    They had not crossed my fate,
The tend'rest hours must have an end,
    And passion has its date.

The softest love grows cold and shy,
    The face so late adored,
Now unregarded passes by,
    Or grows at last abhorred;   20
All things in nature fickle prove,
    See how they glide away;
Think so in time thy hopeless love
    Will die, as flowers decay.

A Song

While, Iris, I at distance gaze,
    And feed my greedy eyes,
That wounded heart, that dies for you,
    Dull gazing can't suffice;

Hope is the food of love-sick minds,
 On that alone 'twill feast,
The nobler part which loves refines,
 No other can digest.

In vain, too nice and charming maid,
 I did suppress my cares;   10
In vain my rising sighs I stayed,
 And stopped my falling tears;
The flood would swell, the tempest rise,
 As my despair came on;
When from her lovely cruel eyes,
 I found I was undone.

Yet at your feet while thus I lie,
 And languish by your eyes,
'Tis far more glorious here to die,
 Than gain another prize.   20
Here let me sigh, here let me gaze,
 And wish at least to find
As raptured nights, and tender days,
 As he to whom you're kind.

Selinda and Cloris, made in an Entertainment at Court

Selinda

As young Selinda led her flock,
Beneath the shelter of a shaded rock,
The melancholy Cloris by,
Thus to the lovely maid did sighing cry.

Cloris

Selinda, you too lightly prize,
The powerful glories of your eyes;

To suffer young Alexis to adore,
Alexis, whom love made my slave before;
I first adorned him with my chains,
He sighed beneath the rigour of my reign;   } 10
And can that conquest now be worth your pain?
A votary you deserve who ne'er knew how,
To any altars but your own to bow.

Selinda

Is it your friendship or your jealousy,
That brings this timely aid to me?
With reason we that empire quit,
Who so much rigour shows,
And 'twould declare more love than wit,
Not to recall his vows.
If beauty could Alexis move,   20
He might as well be mine;
He saw the errors of his love,
He saw how long in vain he strove,
And did your scorn decline;
And, Cloris, I the Gods may imitate,
And humble penitents receive, though late.

Cloris

Mistaken maid, can his devotion prove
Agreeable or true,
Who only offers broken vows of love?
Vows which, Selinda, are my due.   30
How often prostrate at my feet h'as lain,
Imploring pity for his pain?
My heart a thousand ways he strove to win,
Before it let the charming conqueror in;
Ah then how soon the amorous heat was laid!
How soon he broke the vows he made!
Slighting the trophies he had won.
And smiling saw me sigh for being undone.

Selinda

Enough, enough, my dear abandoned maid,
Enough thy eyes, thy sighs, thy tongue have said,   40
In all the groves, on all the plains,
'Mongst all the shepherds, all the swains,
I never saw the charms could move
My yet unconquered heart, to love;
And though a god Alexis were,
He should not rule the empire here.

Cloris

Then from his charming language fly;
Or thou'rt undone as well as I;
The God of Love is sure his friend,
Who taught him all his arts,   50
And when a conquest he designed,
He furnished him with darts;
His quiver, and his gilded bow,
To his assistance brings,
And having given the fatal blow,
Lends him his fleeting wings.
Though not a cottage-slave, can be,
Before the conquest, so submiss as he,
To fold your sheep, to gather flowers,
To pipe and sing, and sigh away your hours;   60
Early your flocks to fragrant meads,
Or cooling shades, and springs he leads;
Weaves garlands, or go seek your lambs,
That struggle from their bleating dams,
Or any humble bus'ness do,
But once a victor, he's a tyrant too.

Selinda

Cloris, such little services would prove
Too mean, to be repaid with love;
A look, a nod, a smile would quit that score,
And she deserves to be undone, that pays a shepherd more. 70

Cloris

His new-blown passion if Selinda scorn,
Alexis may again to me return.

Selinda

Secure thy fears, the vows he makes to me
I send a present, back to thee;

Cloris

Then we will sing, in every grove,
The greatness of your mind, –

Selinda

. . . And I your love.

Both

And all the day,
With pride and joy,
We'll let the neighb'ring shepherds see,
That none like us,
Did e'er express,
The heights of love and amity;
And all the day, &c.

80

A Pindaric to Mr. P. who sings finely

Damon, although you waste in vain
That precious breath of thine,
Where lies a power in every strain,
To take in any other heart, but mine;
Yet do not cease to sing, that I may know,
By what soft charms and arts,
What more than human 'tis you do,

To take, and keep your hearts;
Or have you vowed never to waste your breath,
But when some maid must fall a sacrifice, 10
As Indian priests prepare a death,
For slaves t'adorn their victories,
Your charm's as powerful, if I live,
For I as sensible shall be,
What wound you can, to all that hear you, give,
As if you wounded me;
And shall as much adore your wondrous skill,
As if my heart each dying note could kill.

And yet I should not tempt my fate,
Nor trust my feeble strength, 20
Which does with ev'ry softning note abate
And may at length
Reduce me to the wretched slave I hate;
Tis strange extremity in me,
To venture on a doubtful victory,
Where if you fail, I gain no more,
Than what I had before;
But 'twill certain comfort bring,
If I unconquered do escape from you;
If I can live, and hear you sing, 30
No other forces can my soul subdue;
Sing, Damon, then, and let each shade,
Which with thy heavenly voice is happy made,
Bear witness if my courage be not great,
To hear thee sing, and make a safe retreat.

A Pastoral to Mr. Stafford, Under the Name of Silvio on his Translation of the Death of Camilla: out of Virgil

THIRSIS and AMARILLIS

Thirsis

Why, Amarillis, dost thou walk alone,
And the gay pleasures of the meadows shun?
Why to the silent groves dost thou retire,
When uncompelled by the Suns scorching fire?
Musing with folded arms, and downcast look,
Or pensive yield to thy supporting hook:
Is Damon false? and has his vows betrayed,
And born the trophies to some other maid?

Amarillis

The Gods forbid I should survive to see
The fatal day he were unjust to me.   10
Nor is my courage, or my love so poor
T' outlive that scorned, and miserable hour;
Rather let wolves my new-yeaned lambs devour,
Wither ye verdant grass, dry up ye streams,
And let all nature turn to vast extremes:
In Summer let the boughs be cale and dry,
And now gay flowers the wandring Spring supply,
But with my Damons love, let all that's charming die.

Thirsis

Why then this dull retreat, if he be true,
Or, Amarillis, is the change in you?   20
You love some swains more rich in herds and flocks,
For none can be more powerful in his looks;
His shape, his mien, his hair, his wondrous face,
And on the plains, none dances with his grace;
'Tis true, in piping he does less excel.

Amarillis

The music of his voice can charm as well,
When tuned to words of love, and sighs among,
With the soft tremblings of his bashful tongue,
And, Thirsis, you accuse my faith in vain,
To think it wavering, for another swain;   30
Tis admiration now that fills my soul,
And does ev'n love suspend, if not control.
My thoughts are solemn all, and do appear
With wonder in my eyes, and not despair!
My heart is entertained with silent joys,
And I am pleased above the mirth of noise.

Thirsis

What new-born pleasure can divert you so?
Pray let me hear, that I may wonder too.

Amarillis

Last night, by yonder purling stream I stood,
Pleased with the murmurs of the little flood,   40
Who in its rapid glidings bore away
The fringing flowers, that made the bank so gay,
Which I compared to fickle swains, who invade
First this, then that deceived, and yielding maid:
Whose flattering vows an easy passage find, ⎫
Then unregarded leave 'em far behind,   ⎬
To sigh their ruin to the flying wind.   ⎭
So the soiled flowers their rifled beauties hung,
While the triumphant ravisher passes on.
This while I sighing viewed, I heard a voice   50
That made the woods, the groves, and hills rejoice.
Who echoed back the charming sound again, ⎫
Answering the music of each soft'ning strain, ⎬
And told the wonder over all the plain.   ⎭
Young Silvio 'twas that tuned his happy pipe,
The best that ever graced a shepherd's lip!
Silvio of noble race, yet not disdains

60

To mix his harmony with rustic swains,
To th' humble shades th' illustrious youth resorts,
Shunning the false delights of gaudy courts,   } 60
For the more solid happiness of rural sports.
Courts which his noble father long pursued,
And served till he out-served their gratitude.

Thirsis

Oh Amarillis, let that tale no more
Remembered be on the Arcadian Shore,
Lest mirth should on our meads no more be found,
But Stafford's story should throughout resound,
And fill with pitying cries the echos all around.

Amarillis

Arcadia, keep your peace, but give me leave,
Who knew the heros loyalty, to grieve;   70
Once, Thirsis, by th' Arcadian Kings commands,
I left these shades, to visit foreign lands;
Employed in public toils of state affairs,
Unusual with my sex, or to my years;
There 'twas my chance, so Fortune did ordain,
To see this great, this good, this god-like man:
Brave, pious, loyal, just, without constraint,
The soul all angel, and the man a saint;
His tempered mind no passion e'er inflamed,
But when his king and country were profaned;   80
Then oft I've seen his generous blood o'er spread
His awful face, with a resenting red,
In anger quit the room, and would disdain
To herd with the rebellious publican.
But, Thirsis, 'twould a worshipped volume fill,
If I the heros wondrous life should tell;
His virtues were his crime, like God he bowed
A necessary victim to the frantic crowd;
So a tall shelt'ring oak that long had stood,
The mid-days shade, and glory of the wood;   90

Whose aged boughs a reverence did command,
Fell lopped at last by an ignoble hand:
And all his branches are in pieces torn,
That victors graced, and did the wood adorn.
– With him young Silvio, who composed his joys,
The darling of his soul and of his eyes,
Inheriting the virtues of his sire,
But all his own is his poetic fire;
When young, the Gods of love, and wit did grace
The pointed, promised beauties of his face,   100
Which ripening years did to perfection bring,
And taught him how to love, and how to sing.

Thirsis

But what, dear Amarillis, was the theme
The noble Silvio sung by yonder stream?

Amarillis

Not of the shepherds, nor their rural loves.
The song was glorious though 'twas sung in groves!
Camilla's death the skilful youth inspired,
As if th' heroic Maid his soul had fired;
Such life was in his song, such heat, such flight,
As he had seen the royal Virgin fight.   110
He made her deal her wounds with graceful Art, ⎫
With vigorous air fling the unfailing dart,   ⎬
And formed her courage to his own great heart. ⎭
Never was fighting in our sex a charm,
Till Silvio did the bright Camilla arm;
With noble modesty he shows us how
To be at once Hero and Woman too.
Oh conquering maid! how much thy fame has won, ⎫
In the Arcadian language to be sung,   ⎬
And by a swain so soft, so sweet, so young.   ⎭   120

Thirsis

Well hast thou spoke the noble Silvio's praise,
For I have often heard his charming lays;
Oft has he blessed the shades with strains divine,
Took many a virgin's heart, and ravished mine.
Long may he sing in every field and grove,
And teach the swains to pipe, the maids to love.

Amarillis

Daphnis, and Colin pipe not half so well,
E'en Dion's mighty self he does excel;
As the last lover of the Muses, blessed,
The last and young in love are always best;   130
And she her darling lover does requite
With all the softest arts of noblest wit.

Thirsis

Oh may he dedicate his youth to her!
Thus let 'em live, and love upon the square,
But see Alexis homeward leads his flock,
And browsing goats descend from yonder rock;
The Sun is hasting on to Thetis bed,
See his faint beams have streaked the sky with red.
Let's home ere night approach, and all the way
You shall of Silvio sing, while I will play.   140

Ovid to Julia

A Letter

Fair royal maid, permit a youth undone
To tell you how he drew his ruin on;
By what degrees he took that poison in,
That made him guilty of Prometheus sin;

Who from the Gods durst steal celestial fire,
And though with less success, I did as high aspire.
Oh why ye Gods! was she of mortal race?
And why 'twixt her and me, was there so vast a space?
Why was she not above my passion made
Some star in heaven, or goddess of the shade?   10
And yet my haughty soul could ne'er have bowed
To any beauty, of the common crowd.
None but the brow, that did expect a crown
Could charm or awe me with a smile, or frown;
I had the envy of th' Arcadian plains,
Sought by the nymphs, and bowed to by the swains;
Where I passed, I swept the fields along,
And gathered round me all the gazing throng:
In numerous flocks and herds I did abound,
And when I spread my wanton wishes round,   20
They wanted nothing but my being crowned.
Yet witness all ye spightful powers above,
If my ambition did not spring from love!
Had you my charming Julia been less fair,
Less excellent, less conqu'ring than you are,
I had my glorious loyalty retained,
My noble blood untainted had remained,
Witness ye groves, witness ye sacred powers!
Ye shaded rivers banks, and beds of flowers,
Where the expecting nymphs have past their hours.   30
Witness how oft, all careless of their fame,
They languished for the author of their flame,
And when I came reproached my cold reserve;
Asked for what nymph I did my joys preserve?
What sighing maid was next to be undone?
For whom I dressed, and put my graces on?
And never thought, (tho I feigned every proof
Of tender passion) that I loved enough.
While I with love's variety was cloyed;
Or the faint pleasure like a dream enjoyed.   40
'Twas Julia's brighter eyes my soul alone
With everlasting gust, could feed upon.

From her first bloom my fate I did pursue,
And from the tender fragrant bud, I knew
The charming sweets it promised, when it blew.
This gave me love, and 'twas in vain I tried
The beauty from the Princess to divide;
For he at once must feel, whom you inspire,
A soft ambition, and a haughty fire,
And hopes the natural aid of young desire.   50
My unconsidering passion had not yet
Thought your illustrious birth for mine too great,
'Twas love that I pursued, vast love that leads
Sometimes the equalled slave, to princes beds.
But I forgot that sacred flame must rest
In your bright soul, that makes th' adorer blest;
Your generous fire alone must you subdue,
And raise the humbler lover up to you;
Yet if by chance m' ambition met a stop,
By any thought that checked m' advancing hope,   60
This new one straight would all the rest confound,
How ev'ry coxcomb aimed at being crowned;
The vain young fool with all his mothers parts,
(Who wanted wit enough for little arts,)
With crowds, and unmatched nonsense, lays a claim
To th' glorious title of a sovereign;
And when for gods such wretched things set up,
Was it so great a crime in me to hope?
No laws of Heaven, or man my vows reprove;
There is no treason in ambitious love.   70
That sacred antidote, i'th' poisoned cup,
Quells the contagion of each little drop,
I bring no forces, but my sighs and tears,
My languishments, my soft complaints and prayers,
Artillery which I ne'er sent in vain,
Nor failed where'er addressed, to wound with pain
Here, only here! rebated they return,
Meeting the solid armour of your scorn;
Scorn! By the Gods! I any thing could bear,
The rough fatigues and storms of dangerous war;   80

Long winters marches, or the summer heat,
Nay even in battle from the foe defeat;
Scars on my face, scars, whose dull recompence,
Would ne'er atone for what they rob from thence.
Scandal of coward, nay half witted too,
Or siding with the pardoned rebel crew;
Or any thing but scorn, – and yet frown on,
Your slave was destined thus to be undone.
You the avenging Deity appear,
And I a victim fall to all the injured fair.   90

To Damon

To inquire of him if he could tell me by the style, who writ me a
copy of verses that came to me in an unknown hand

Oh, Damon, if thou ever wert
  That certain friend thou hast professed,
Relieve the rantings of my heart,
  Restore me to my wonted rest.

  Late in the Silvian grove I sat,
  Free as the air, and calm as that;
  For as no winds the boughs oppressed,
  No storms of love were in my breast.
  A long adieu I'd bid to that
  Ere since Amintas proved ingrate.   10
  And with indifference, or disdain,
I looked around upon the plain
And worth my favour found no sighing swain.
  But oh, my Damon, all in vain
    I triumphed in security,
  In vain absented from the plain.
    The wanton God his power to try
  In lone recesses makes us yield,

66

As well as in the open field;
For where no human thing was found   20
My heedless heart reeeived a wound.
Assist me, shepherd, or I die,
Help to unfold this mystery.

No swain was by, no flattering nymph was near,
Soft tales of love to whisper in my ear.
    In sleep, no dream my fancy fired
With images, my waking wish desired.
    No fond idea filled my mind;
Nor to the faithless sex one thought inclined;
    I sighed for no deceiving youth,   30
    Who forfeited his vows and truth;
    I waited no assigning swain
    Whose disappointment gave me pain.
    My fancy did no prospect take
    Of conquests I designed to make.
    No snares for lovers I had laid,
    Nor was of any snare afraid.
    But calm and innocent I sate,   ⎫
    Content with my indifferent fate.   ⎬
    (A medium, I confess, I hate.)   ⎭   40
    For when the mind so cool is grown   ⎫
    As neither love nor hate to own,   ⎬
    The life but dully lingers on.   ⎭

    Thus in the midst of careless thought,
    A paper to my hand was brought.
    What hidden charms were lodged within,
    To my unwary eyes unseen,
    Alas! no human thought can guess;
    But ho! it robbed me of my peace.
    A philter 'twas, that darted pain   50
    Through every pleased and trembling vein.
    A stratagem, to send a dart
    By a new way into the heart,
    Th' ignoble policy of love

67

By a clandestine means to move.
Which possibly the instrument ⎫
Did ne'er design to that intent, ⎬
But only form, and complement. ⎭
While Love did the occasion take
And hid beneath his flowers a snake,   60
O'er every line did poison fling,
In every word he lurked a sting.
So matrons are, by demons charms,
Though harmless, capable of harms.

 The verse was smooth, the thought was fine,
 The fancy new, the wit divine.
But filled with praises of my face and eyes,
My verse, and all those usual flatteries
 To me as common as the air;
Nor could my vanity procure my care.   70
 All which as things of course are writ
 And less to show esteem than wit.
 But here was some strange something more
 Than ever flattered me before;
 My heart was by my eyes misled:
 I blushed and trembled as I read.
 And every guilty look confessed
 I was with new surprise oppressed.
 From every view I felt a pain
 And by the soul, I drew the swain.   80
 Charming as fancy could create
Fine as his poem, and as soft as that.

 I drew him all the heart could move,
 I drew him all that women love.
 And such a dear idea made
 As has my whole repose betrayed.
 Pygmalion thus his image formed,
And for the charms he made, he sighed and burned.

Oh thou that know'st each shepherds strains
That pipes and sings upon the plains;   } 90
Inform me where the youth remains.
The spiteful paper bear no name,
Nor can I guess from whom it came,
Or if at least a guess I found,
Twas not t'instruct but to confound.

To Alexis in Answer to his Poem against Fruition

ODE

Ah hapless sex! who bear no charms,
But what like lightning flash and are no more,
    False fires sent down for baneful harms,
Fires which the fleeting lover feebly warms
    And given like past debauches o'er,
    Like songs that please (though bad) when new,
    But learned by heart neglected grew.

In vain did Heav'n adorn the shape and face
With beauties which by angels forms it drew:
In vain the mind with brighter glories grace,   10
While all our joys are stinted to the space
    Of one betraying interview,
With one surrender to the eager will
We 're short-lived nothing, or a real ill.

Since man with that inconstancy was born,
To love the absent, and the present scorn,
    Why do we deck, why do we dress
    For such a short-lived happiness?
    Why do we put attraction on,
Since either way tis we must be undone?   20

They fly if honour take our part,
  Our virtue drives 'em o'er the field.
We lose 'em by too much desert,
  And Oh! they fly us if we yield.
Ye Gods! is there no charm in all the fair
To fix this wild, this faithless, wanderer?

Man! our great business and our aim,
  For whom we spread our fruitless snares,
No sooner kindles the designing flame,
  But to the next bright object bears   30
The trophies of his conquest and our shame:
  Inconstancy's the good supreme,
The rest is airy notion, empty dream!

Then, heedless nymph, be ruled by me
  If e'er your swain the bliss desire;
Think like Alexis he may be
  Whose wished possession damps his fire;
The roving youth in every shade
Has left some sighing and abandoned maid,
For tis a fatal lesson he has learned,   40
After fruition ne'er to be concerned.

To Alexis, On his saying, I loved a Man that talked much

Alexis, since you'll have it so
  I grant I am impertinent.
And till this moment did not know
  Through all my life what 'twas I meant;
Your kind opinion was th' unflattering glass,
In which my mind found how deformed it was.

In your clear sense which knows no art,
  I saw the error of my soul;

70

And all the feebless of my heart,
   With one reflection you control,   10
Kind as a god, and gently you chastise,
By what you hate, you teach me to be wise.

Impertinence, my sexes shame,
   (Which has so long my life pursued,)
You with such modesty reclaim
   As all the woman has subdued,
To so divine a power what must I owe,
That renders me so like the perfect – you?

That conversable thing I hate
   Already with a just disdain,   20
Who prides himself upon his prate
   And is of word, (that nonsense,) vain;
When in your few appears such excellence,
They have reproached and charmed me into sense.

For ever may I list'ning sit,
   Though but each hour a word be born:
I would attend the coming wit,
   And bless what can so well inform:
Let the dull world henceforth to words be damned,
I'm into nobler sense than talking shamed.   30

On Desire

A Pindaric

What art thou, oh! thou new-found pain?
From what infection dost thou spring?
Tell me, – oh! tell me, thou enchanting thing,
   Thy nature, and thy name;
Inform me by what subtle art,
   What powerful influence,

You got such vast dominion in a part
Of my unheeded, and unguarded, heart,
That fame and honour cannot drive ye thence.

Oh! mischievous usurper of my peace;   10
Oh! soft intruder on my solitude,
   Charming disturber of my ease,
   Thou hast my nobler fate pursued,
And all the glories of my life subdued.

    Thou haunt'st my inconvenient hours;
The business of the day, nor silence of the night,
     That should to cares and sleep invite,
    Can bid defiance to thy conquering powers.

    Where hast thou been this live-long age
     That from my birth till now,   20
   Thou never could'st one thought engage,
Or charm my soul with the uneasy rage
That made it all its humble feebles know?

    Where wert thou, oh, malicious spright,
    When shining honour did invite?
    When interest called, then thou wert shy,
Nor to my aid one kind propension brought,
    Nor would'st inspire one tender thought,
    When princes at my feet did lie.

When thou could'st mix ambition with thy joy,   30
Then peevish phantom, thou wert nice and coy,
    Not beauty could invite thee then
    Nor all the arts of lavish men;
Not all the powerful rhetoric of the tongue
    Not sacred wit could charm thee on;
    Not the soft play that lovers make,
Nor sigh could fan thee to a fire,
Not pleading tears, nor vows could thee awake,
Or warm the unformed something – to desire.

Oft I've conjured thee to appear   40
   By youth, by love, by all their powers,
   Have searched and sought thee everywhere,
In silent groves, in lonely bowers:
On flow'ry beds where lovers wishing lie,
     In sheltering woods where sighing maids
     To their assigning shepherds hie,
And hide their blushes in the gloom of shades:
     Yet there, even there though youth assailed,
Where beauty prostrate lay and fortune wooed,
My heart insensible to neither bowed,   50
The lucky aid was wanting to prevail.

In courts I sought thee then, thy proper sphere
     But thou in crowds wert stifled there,
Int'rest did all the loving business do,
Invites the youths and wins the virgins too.
Or if by chance some heart thy empire own
(Ah power ingrate!) the slave must be undone.

Tell me, thou nimble fire, that dost dilate
     Thy mighty force through every part,
What god, or human power, did thee create   60
     In my, till now, unfacil' heart?
Art thou some welcome plague sent from above
     In this dear form, this kind disguise?
     Or the false offspring of mistaken love,
     Begot by some soft thought that faintly strove,
With the bright piercing beauties of Lysanders eyes?

    Yes, yes, tormentor, I have found thee now;
    And found to whom thou dost thy being owe,
      'Tis thou the blushes dost impart,
      For thee this languishment I wear,   70
      'Tis thou that tremblest in my heart
      When the dear shepherd does appear,
      I faint, I die with pleasing pain,
      My words intruding sighing break

Whene'er I touch the charming swain
Whene'er I gaze, whene'er I speak.
Thy conscious fire is mingled with my love,
 As in the sanctified abodes
 Misguided worshippers approve
The mixing idol with their gods.   80

In vain, alas! in vain I strive
With errors, which my soul do please and vex,
 For superstition will survive,
 Purer religion to perplex.

Oh! tell me you, philosophers, in love,
That can its burning feverish fits control,
 By what strange arts you cure the soul,
 And the fierce calenture remove?

Tell me, ye fair ones, that exchange desire,
 How tis you hid the kindling fire.   90
 Oh! would you but confess the truth,
It is not real virtue makes you nice:
But when you do resist the pressing youth,
'Tis want of dear desire, to thaw the virgin ice.
 And while your young adorers lie
All languishing and hopeless at your feet,
 Raising new trophies to your chastity,
 Oh tell me, how you do remain discreet?
 How you suppress the rising sighs,
And the soft yielding soul that wishes in your eyes?   100
 While to th'admiring crowd you nice are found;
 Some dear, some secret, youth that gives the wound
 Informs you, all your virtue's but a cheat
  And honour but a false disguise,
 Your modesty a necessary bait
 To gain the dull repute of being wise.

Deceive the foolish world – deceive it on,
 And veil your passions in your pride;

But now I've found your feebles by my own,
From me the needful fraud you cannot hide.   110
    Though tis a mighty power must move
    The soul to this degree of love,
And though with virtue I the world perplex,
Lysander finds the weakness of my sex,
So Helen while from Theseus arms she fled,
To charming Paris yields her heart and bed.

On the first discovery of falseness in Amintas

Make haste! make haste! my miserable soul,
    To some unknown and solitary grove,
Where nothing may thy languishment control
    Where thou may'st never hear the name of Love.
Where unconfined, and free, as whispering air,
Thou may'st caress and welcome thy despair:

Where no dissembled complaisance may veil
    The griefs with which, my soul, thou art oppressed,
But dying, breath thyself out in a tale
    That may declare the cause of thy unrest: 10
The toils of death 'twill render far more light
And soon convey thee to the shades of night.

Search then, my soul, some unfrequented place,
    Some place that nature meant her own repose:
When she herself withdrew from human race,
    Displeased with wanton lovers vows and oaths.
Where Sol could never dart a busy ray,
And where the softer winds ne'er met to play.

By the sad purling of some rivulet
    O'er which the bending yew and willow grow,   20
That scarce the glimmerings of the day permit,

To view the melancholy banks below,
Where dwells no noise but what the murmurs make,
When the unwilling stream the shade forsakes.

There on a bed of moss and new-fall'n leaves,
    Which the triumphant trees once proudly bore,
Though now thrown off by every wind that breaths,
    Despised by what they did adorn before,
And who, like useless me, regardless lie
While springing beauties do the boughs supply.   30

There lay thee down, my soul, and breath thy last,
    And calmly to the unknown regions fly;
But ere thou dost thy stock of life exhaust,
    Let the ungrateful know, why tis you die.
Perhaps the gentle winds may chance to bear
Thy dying accents to Amintas ear.

Breath out thy passion; tell him of his power
    And how thy flame was once by him approved.
How soon as wished he was thy conqueror,
    No sooner spoke of love, but was beloved.   40
His wonderous eyes, what weak resistance found,
While every charming word begat a wound?

Here thou wilt grow impatient to be gone,
    And through my willing eyes will silent pass,
Into the stream that gently glides along,
    But stay thy hasty flight, (my soul,) alas,
A thought more cruel will thy flight secure,
Thought, that can no admittance give to cure.

Think, how the prostrate infidel now lies,
    An humble suppliant at anothers feet,   50
Think, while he begs for pity from her eyes.
    He sacrifices thee without regret.
Think, how the faithless treated thee last night,
And then, my tortured soul, assume thy flight.

To the fair Clarinda, who made Love to me, imagined more than Woman

Fair lovely maid, or if that title be
Too weak, too feminine for nobler thee,
Permit a name that more approaches truth:
And let me call thee, lovely charming youth.
This last will justify my soft complaint,
While that may serve to lessen my constraint;
And without blushes I the youth pursue,
When so much beauteous woman is in view.
Against thy charms we struggle but in vain ⎫
With thy deluding form thou giv'st us pain, ⎬   10
While the bright nymph betrays us to the swain. ⎭
In pity to our sex sure thou wert sent,
That we might love, and yet be innocent:
For sure no crime with thee we can commit;
Or if we should – thy form excuses it.
For who, that gathers fairest flowers believes
A snake lies hid beneath the fragrant leaves.

   Thou beauteous wonder of a different kind,
Soft Cloris with the dear Alexis joined;
Whene'er the manly part of thee, would plead   20
Thou tempts us with the image of the maid,
While we the noblest passions do extend
The love to Hermes, Aphrodite the friend.

Verses designed by Mrs. A. Behn to be sent to a fair Lady, that desired she would absent herself to cure her Love. Left unfinished

In vain to woods and deserts I retire, ⎫
To shun the lovely charmer I admire, ⎬
Where the soft breezes do but fan my fire! ⎭

In vain in grotto's dark unseen I lie,
Love pierces where the Sun could never spy.
No place, no art his Godhead can exclude,
The dear distemper reigns in solitude:
Distance, alas, contributes to my grief;
No more, of what fond lovers call, relief
Than to the wounded hind does sudden flight   10
From the chaste Goddesses pursuing sight:
When in the heart the fatal shaft remains,
And darts the venom through our bleeding veins.
If I resolve no longer to submit
My self a wretched conquest to your wit,
More swift than fleeting shades, ten thousand charms
From your bright eyes that rebel thought disarms:
The more I struggled to my grief I found
My self in Cupid's chains more surely bound:
Like birds in nets, the more I strive, I find   20
My self the faster in the snare confined.

On a Pin that hurt Amintas' Eye

Injurious Pin, how durst thou steal so nigh?
To touch, nay worse, to hurt his precious eye.
Base instrument, so ill thou'st played thy part,
Wounding his eye, thou'st wounded my poor heart,
And for each pitied drop his eye did shed,
My sympathizing heart a thousand bled:
Too daring pin, was there no tincture good,
To bathe thy point, but my Amintas' blood?

Could thy ambition teach thee so to sin?
Was that a place for thee to revel in?   10
'Twas there thy mistress had designed to be,
And must she find a rival too in thee?
Cursed fate! that I should harbour thee so long,

And thou at last conspire to do me wrong:
Though well I knew thy nature to be rude,
And all thy kin full of ingratitude,
I little thought thou wouldst presume so far,
To aim thy malice at so bright a star.

Now all the service thou canst render me
Will never recompense this injury.   20

Well, get thee gone – for thou shalt never more
Have power to hurt what I so much adore.
Hence from my sight, and mayst thou ever lie
A crooked object to each scornful eye.

For Damon, being asked a Reason for his Love

You ask me, Phillis, why I still pursue,
    And court no other nymph but you;
And why with looks and sighs I still betray
    A passion which I dare not say.
'Tis all, because I do: you ask me why,
And with a woman's reason, I reply.

You ask what argument I have to prove,
    That my unrest proceeds from love,
You'll not believe my passion till you know,
    A better reason why 'tis so.   10
Then, Phillis, let this reason go for one,
I know I love because my reason's gone.

You say a love like mine must needs declare
    The object so beloved not fair;
That neither wit nor beauty in her dwell,
    Whose lover can no reason tell,
What 'tis that he adores, and why he burns:
Phillis, let those give such that have returns.

And by the very reasons that you use,
    Damon might justly you accuse;   20
Why do you scorn, and with proud disdain
    Receive the vow, and slight the swain?
You say you cannot love, you know no cause:
May I not prove my love by your own laws?

Am not I youthful, and as gay a swain,
    As e'er appeared upon the plain?
Have I not courted you with all th' address
    An am'rous shepherd could profess?
And add to this, my flocks and herds are great,
But Phillis only can my joy complete.   30

Yet you no reason for your coldness give,
    And 'tis but just you should believe
That all your beauties unadorned by art,
    Have hurt and not obliged my heart.
Be kind to that, my hearty vows return
And then I'll tell you why, for what I burn.

A Letter to the Earl of Kildare, dissuading him from marrying Moll Howard

My Lord,
We pity such as are by tempest lost,
And those by Fortune's blind disposal crossed;
But when men see, and may the danger shun,
Yet headlong into certain ruin run:
To pity such, must needs be ridicule;
Do not (my Lord) be that unpitied fool.

There's a report, which round the Town is spread,
The famed Moll Howard you intend to wed;
If it be true, my Lord, then guard your head:
Horns, horns, by wholesale, will adorn your brows,   10

If e'er you make that rampant whore your spouse.
Think on the lewd debauches of her life;
Then tell me, if she's fit to be your wife.
She that to quench her lustful, hot desire,
Has kissed with dukes, lords, knights, and country squire; }
Nay, grooms and footmen have been clawed off by her.

Whoring has all her life-time been her trade,
And D—set says, she is an exc'llent bawd:
But finding both will not defray expense,
She lately is become an evidence;   20
Swears against all that won't her lust supply,
And says, they're false as Hell to monarchy.

You had a wife; but, rest her soul, she's dead,
By whom your Lordship by the nose was led:
And will you run into that noose again,
To be the greatest monster among men?
Think on the horns that will adorn your head,
And the diseases that will fill your bed:
Pox upon pox, most horrid and most dire!
And ulcers filled with Hell's eternal fire.   30

Forbear therefore, and call your senses home;
Let reason love's blind passion overcome:
For, if you make this base report once true,
You'll wound your honour, purse, and body too.

To Mrs. Price

My Dear,
   In your last, you admired how I could pass my time so long
in the country: I am sorry your taste is so depraved, as not to
relish a country-life. Now I think there's no satisfaction to be
found amidst an urban throng (as Mr. Bayes calls it).

The peaceful place where gladly I resort,
Is freed from noisy factions of the court:
There joyed with viewing o'er the rural scene,
Pleased with the meadows ever green,
The woods and groves with tuneful anger move,
And nought is heard but gentle sighs of love:
The nymphs and swains for rural sports prepare,
And each kind youth diverts his smiling fair.
But if by chance is found a flinty maid,
Whose cruel eyes has shepherds hearts betrayed,   10
In other climes a refuge she must find,
Banished from hence society of kind.
Here gentle Isis, with a bridegroom's haste,
Glides to o'ertake the Thame, as fair, as chaste;
Then mixed embracing, they together fly;
They live together, and together die.
Here ev'ry object adds to our delight,
Calm is our day, and peaceful is our night.
Then, kind Æmilia, fly that hated town,
Where's not a moment thou canst call thy own: 20
Haste for to meet a happiness divine,
And share the pleasures I count only mine.

*A Poem Humbly Dedicated to the Great Pattern of Piety
and Virtue Catherine Queen Dowager on the Death of
her Dear Lord and Husband King Charles II*

Pardon! Oh sacred mourner! that we paid
Our first sad tributes to the royal dead;
Which did our souls to rending sighs convert,
Drained our fixed eyes, and pierced the bleeding heart;
And for a loss that Heav'n can ne'er redress,
Our raging griefs were rude in their excess:
Which, while with wild devotion we pursue
Ev'n Heav'n neglected lay, ev'n sacred You:

Our own dire fates did all our tears employ,
Griefs have such self-interest too as well as joy.   10
But when such sacrifice from us is due,   ⎫
What must the mighty loss exact from you,   ⎬
Who mourn a king, and dear loved husband too!   ⎭
How shall we measure that vast tide of woe,
That did your royal breaking heart o'erflow?
And almost, with a high imperious force,
Bore down the banks of life in its too rapid course.
Your languishments and sorrows, who repeats,   ⎫
Or by his own, on yours a value sets,   ⎬
Compares deep seas to wand'ring rivulets;   ⎭   20
Who though a while in their own meads they stray,
Lose their young streams at last in the unbounded sea.
Should all the nations tenderest griefs combine,   ⎫
And all our pangs in one vast body join,   ⎬
They could not sigh with agonies like thine.   ⎭
That you survive, is Heav'ns peculiar care,
To charm our grief, and heal our wild despair;
While we to Charles's sacred relict bow,
Half the great monarch we adore in you:
The rest, our natural devotions grant;   30
We bless the Queen, and we invoke the Saint:
Nor fades your light with Englands worshipped sun,
Your joys were set, but still your glory shone:
And with a lustre that shall still increase,
When worlds shall be no more, and Natures self shall cease;
For never in one mortal frame did join
A fortitude and virtue more divine:
Witness the steady graces of your soul   ⎫
When charged by perjuries so black and foul,   ⎬
As did all laws, both human and divine control.   ⎭   40
When Heaven (to make the heroine understood,   ⎫
And Hell itself permitted loose abroad,)   ⎬
Gave you the patience of a suffering god.   ⎭
So our blest Saviour his reproaches bore,   ⎫
When piercing thorns His sacred temples wore,   ⎬
And stripes compelled the rich redeeming gore.   ⎭

Your precious life alone, the fiends disdained,
To murder home, your virtue they prophaned;
By plots so rude, so hellish a pretence,
As ev'n would call in question Providence: 50
Or why avenging thunder did not strike
Those cursed hands durst touch the sacred Ark;
But as where long the Sun is set in night,
They with more joy salute the breaking light,
Heav'n cast this cloud before your radiant beams,
To prove their force by contrary extremes;
The nations all with new devotion bow,
To glories never understood till now:
'Twas majesty and beauty awed before,
But now the brighter virtue they adore.   60

This the great Lord of all your vows beheld,
And with disdain Hells baffled rage repelled;
He knew your soul and the soft angel there,
And long (kind rivals) did that empire share;
And all your tears, your pleading eloquence,
Were needless treasures, lavished to convince
The adorer of your known, and sacred innocence.
When not for life the royal supplicant moved,
But his belief, whom more than life she loved;
From whom, if e'er a frown she could receive,   70
'Twas when she doubted that he could believe;
While he repeats the dear confirming vows,
And the first soft addressing lover shows.

By your reflecting smiles the world was gay,
Faction was fled, and universal joy
Made the glad business of the welcome day.
Ah! too secure we basked beneath the Sun,
And little thought his race so near was run,
But as if Phaeton had usurped its rule,
In the full brightness of its course it fell,   80
Whilst all the frighted world with wonder gazed,
And Nature at her own disorder stood amazed:

84

While you, ah pious mourner did prepare
To offer up to Heav'n your early prayer;
You little thought 'twould meet your dear-loved monarch there:
But on the wings of Death the news approached,
And e'en destroyed the wondring sense it touched;
O mighty heav'n-born soul! that could support
So like a god! this cruel first effort!
Without the feebler sexes mean replies,   90
The April tributes of their tears and cries.
Your valued loss a noisy grief disdained
Fixed in the heart, no outward sign remained;
Though the soft woman bowed and died within;
Without, majestic grace maintained the Queen!
Yet swiftly to the royal bed you fly,   ⎫
Like short-lived lightning from the parted sky; ⎬
Whose new-born motions do but flash and die.   ⎭
Such vig'rous life ne'er moved your steps before,
But here——they sunk beneath the weight they bore.   100
Princes we more than human do allow,   ⎫
You must have been above an angel too;   ⎬
Had you resisted this sad scene of woe;   ⎭
So the blest Virgin at the worlds great loss,
Came, and beheld, then fainted at the Cross.

    Methinks I see, you like the Queen of Heav'n,
To whom all patience and all grace was giv'n;
When the great Lord of Life Himself was laid
Upon her lap, all wounded, pale, and dead;
Transpierced with anguish, ev'n to death transformed,   110
So she bewailed her God! so sighed, so mourned;
So His blest image in her heart remained,
So His blest memory o'er her soul still reigned!
She lived the sacred victim to deplore,
And never knew, or wished a pleasure more.

    But when to your apartment you were brought,
And grief was fortified with second thought;
O how it burst whate'er its force withstood,

Sighed to a storm, and swelled into a flood;
Courage, which is but a peculiar art   120
By Honour taught; where Nature has no part:
Whene'er the soul to fiercer passions yield,
It ceases to be brave and quits the field;
Does the abandoned sinking heart expose
Amidst ten thousand griefs, its worst of foes.

   Your court, what dismal majesty it wears,
Infecting all around with sighs and tears;
No soul so dull, so insensible is found,
Without concern to tread the hallowed ground;
Awful, and silent, all the rooms of state,   130
And emptiness is solemn there, and great;
No more recesses of the sprightly gay,
But a retreat for death, from noise and day:
Echoes from room to room we may pursue,
Soft sighs may hear, but nothing is in view;
Like groves enchanted, where wrecked lovers lie,
And breath their moans to all the passers-by;
Who no kind aids to their relief can bring,
But echo back their pitying sighs again.
But the mysterious sanctum is concealed,   140
To vulgar eyes that must not be revealed;
To your alcove your splendours you confine,
Like a bright saint veiled in a sable shrine;
As the chaste Goddess of the silent night,
You reign alone, retired from gaudy light;
So mourning Cynthia with her starry train,
Wept the sad fate of her loved sleeping swain.

To Henry Higden, Esq; on his Translation
of the Tenth Satire of Juvenal

I

I know you, and I must confess
    From sense so celebrated, and so true,
        Wit so uncommon, and so new,
        As that which always shines in you;
            I could expect no less.
    'Tis great, 'tis just, 'tis noble all!
    Right spirit of the original;
    No scattered spark, no glimmering beams,
    As in some pieces here and there,
Through a dark glade of duller numbers gleams.   10
But tis all fire! all glittering everywhere
Grateful instruction that can never fail,
        To please and charm, even while you rail.
        By arts thus gentle and severe
The Powers divine first made their mortals wise;
The soft reproach they did with reverence bear;
While they adored the God that did chastise.

II

Perhaps there may be found some carping wit,
    May blame the measures of thy lines,
And cry, – Not so the Roman poet writ;   20
Who dressed his satire in more lofty rhymes.
But thou for thy instructor Nature chose,
That first best principle of poetry;
And to thy subject didst thy verse dispose,
While in harmonious union both agree.
Had the great Bard thy properer numbers viewed,
He would have layed his stiff heroics by,
And this more gay, more airy path pursued,
That so much better leads to raillery.

Wit is no more than nature well expressed;   30
  And he fatigues and toils in vain
  With rigid labours, breaks his brain,
That has familiar thought in lofty numbers dressed.

III

True to his sense and to his charming wit,
Thou everywhere hast kept an equal pace:
  All his brisk turns exactly hit,
Justly maintained his humour and his grace:
And with the language hast not changed the face:
   Great Juvenal in every line,
   True Roman still o'er all does shine;   40
But in the British garb appears most fine.

IV

Long did the learned Author search to find
The vice and vanity of humankind:
Long he observed, nor did observe in vain;
  In every differing humour found
  Even there where virtue did abound,
   Some mortal frailties reign.
  Philosophers he saw were proud
  Of dull-affected poverty:
  Senators cringing to the crowd   50
  For trifling popularity:
The judge reviles the criminal at bar,
  And now because old ages ice
Has chilled the ardour of his willing vice,
Snarls at those youthful follies which he cannot shun.
From the vain-keeping 'squire and cullied lord;
The fawning courtier, states-man's broken word:
Down to the flattering, jilting courtesan,
And the more faithless cozening citizen,
The tricks of court and state to him were known;   60
And all the vices veiled beneath the gown,

From the sharp pulpit to the blunted stall,
He knew, and gently did reproach them all.

V

If Rome that kept the lesser world in awe,
Wanted a Juvenal to give them law,
How much more we who stocked with knave and fool,
Have turned the nation into ridicule.
The dire contagion spreads to each degree
      Of wild debauchery.
    The mad infected youth make haste   70
To day their fortunes, health, and reason waste:
      The fop, a tamer sort of tool
        Who dresses, talks, and loves, by rule;
Has long for a fine person passed.
Block-heads will pass for wits, and write,
And some for brave, who ne'er could fight.
Women for chaste, whose knack of cant
Boasts of the virtues that they want:
Cry faugh – at words and actions innocent,
And make that naughty that was never meant: 80
That vain-affected hypocrite shall be
In satire shamed to honest sense by thee.
'Tis thou, an English Juvenal, alone,
To whom all vice, and every virtue's known:
Thou that like Judah's king through all hast passed,
And found that all's but vanity at last;
'Tis you alone the discipline can use,
Who dare at once be bold, severe, and kind;
Soften rough satire with thy gentler Muse,
And force a blush at least, where you can't change the mind.90

On the Death of E. Waller, Esq;

How, to thy sacred memory, shall I bring
(Worthy thy fame) a grateful offering?
I, who by toils of sickness, am become
Almost as near as thou art to a tomb?
While every soft, and every tender strain
Is ruffled and ill-natured grown with pain.
But, at thy name, my languished Muse revives,
And a new spark in the dull ashes strives.
I hear thy tuneful verse, thy song divine,
And am inspired by every charming line.　　　　　　10
But, Oh!——
What inspiration, at the second hand,
Can an immortal elegy command?
Unless, like pious offerings, mine should be
Made sacred, being consecrate to thee.
Eternal, as thy own almighty verse,
Should be those trophies that adorn thy hearse.
The thought illustrious, and the fancy young;⎫
The wit sublime, the judgment fine and strong;⎬
Soft, as thy notes to Sacharissa sung.　　　　　⎭　20
Whilst mine, like transitory flowers, decay,
That come to deck thy tomb a short-lived day.
Such tributes are, like tenures, only fit
To show from whom we hold our right to wit.
　　Hail, wondrous bard, whose heav'n-born Genius first
My infant Muse, and blooming fancy nursed.
With thy soft food of love I first began,
Then fed on nobler panegyric strain,
Numbers seraphic! and at every view,
My soul extended, and much larger grew:　　　　30
Where'er I read, new raptures seized my blood;
Me thought I heard the language of a god.
　　Long did the untuned world in ign'rance stray,⎫
Producing nothing that was great and gay,　　　⎬
Till taught by thee, the true poetic way.　　　　⎭
Rough were the tracts before, dull and obscure;

Nor pleasure, nor instruction could procure.
Their thoughtless labour could no passion move;
Sure, in that age, the poets knew not Love:
That charming God, like apparitions, then,   40
Was only talked on, but ne'er seen by men:
Darkness was o'er the Muses land displayed,
And even the Chosen Tribe unguided strayed.
'Till, by thee rescued from th' Egyptian night, ⎫
They now look up, and view the God of light, ⎬
That taught them how to love, and how to write; ⎭
And to enhance the blessing which Heav'n lent,
When for our great instructor thou wert sent,
Large was thy life, but yet thy glories more; ⎫
And, like the Sun, didst still dispense the power, ⎬   50
Producing something wondrous ev'ry hour: ⎭
And in thy circulatory course, didst see
The very life and death of poetry.
Thou saw'st the Generous Nine neglected lie,
None list'ning to their heav'nly harmony;
The world being grown to that low ebb of sense
To disesteem the noblest excellence;
And no encouragement to prophets shown,
Who in past ages got so great renown.
Though Fortune elevated thee above   60
Its scanty gratitude, or fickle love;
Yet, sullen with the world, untired by age,
Scorning th' unthinking crowd, thou quitt'st the stage.

A Congratulatory Poem to her Sacred Majesty
Queen Mary, upon her Arrival in England

While my sad Muse the darkest covert sought,
To give a loose to melancholy thought;
Oppressed and sighing with the heavy weight
Of an unhappy dear loved monarch's fate;

A lone retreat, on Thames's brink she found,
With murmuring osiers fringed, and bending willows crowned,
Through the thick shade could dart no cheerful ray,
Nature dwelt here as in disdain of day:
Content, and pleased with nobler solitude,
No wood-gods, fawns, nor loves did here intrude,   10
Nor nests for wanton birds, the glade allows;
Scarce the soft winds were heard amongst the boughs.

   While thus she lay resolved to tune no more
Her fruitless songs on Britain's faithless shore,
All on a sudden through the woods there rung,
Loud sounds of joy that Io pæans sung.
Maria! blest Maria! was the theme,
Great Britain's happy genius, and her Queen.

   The river nymphs their crystal courts forsake,
Curl their blue locks, and shelly trumpets take.   20
And the surprising news along the shore,
In raptured songs the wondring virgins bore;
Whilst mourning Echo now forgot her sighs,
And sung the new taught anthem to the skies.

   All things in nature, a new face put on,
Thames with harmonious purlings glides along,
And tells her ravished banks, she lately bore
A prize more great than all her hidden store,
Or all the Sun it self e'er saw before.
The brooding Spring, her fragrant bloom sent out,   30
Scattering her early perfumes round about;
No longer waits the lazy teeming hours,
But ere her time produced her odorous flowers;
Maria's eyes anticipate the May,
And life inspired beyond the God of day.

   The Muses all upon this theme divine,
Tuned their best lays, the Muses all, but mine;

Sullen with stubborn loyalty she lay,
And saw the world its eager homage pay,
While Heav'n and Earth on the new scene looked gay.   40
But Oh! what human fortitude can be
Sufficient to resist a deity?
Even our allegiance here, too feebly pleads,
The change in so divine a form persuades;
Maria with the Sun has equal force,
No opposition stops her glorious course,
Her pointed beams through all a passage find,
And fix their rays triumphant in the mind.

And now I wished among the crowds to adore,
And constant wishing did increase my power;   50
From every thought a new-born reason came
Which fortified by bright Maria's fame,
Inspired my Genius with new life and flame,

And thou, great Lord, of all my vows, permit
My Muse who never failed obedience yet,
To pay her tribute at Maria's Feet,
Maria so divine a part of you,
Let me be just – but just with honour too.

Resolved, she joined her chorus with the throng,
And to the listning groves Maria's virtues sung;   60
Maria all enchanting, gay and young.

All hail illustrious daughter of a king,
Shining without, and glorious all within,
Whose eyes beyond your scantier power give laws,
Command the world, and justify the cause;
Nor to secure you empire needs more arms
Than your resistless, and all conquering charms;
Minerva thus alone, old Troy sustained,
Whilst her blest image with three gods remained;
But Oh! your form and manner to relate,   70
The envying fair as soon may imitate,
'Tis all engaging sweet, 'tis all surprising great;

A thousand beauties triumph in your air,
Like those of soft young loves your smiles appear,
And to th' unguarded hearts, as dangerous are.   }

    All natures charms are opened in your face,
You look, you talk, with more than human grace;
All that is wit, all that is eloquence,
The births of finest thought and noblest sense,
Easy and natural from your language break,   80
And 'tis eternal music when you speak;
Through all no formal nicety is seen,
But free and generous your majestic mien,   }
In every motion, every part a queen;
All that is great and lovely in the sex,
Heav'n did in this one glorious wonder fix.
Appelis thus to dress the Queen of Love,
Robbed the whole race, a goddess to improve.

    Yet if with sighs we view that lovely face,
And all the lines of your great father's trace,   90
Your virtues should forgive, while we adore
That face that awes, and charms our hearts the more;
But if the Monarch in your looks we find,
Behold him yet more glorious in your mind;
'Tis there his God-like attributes we see.
A gracious sweetness, affability,   }
A tender mercy and true piety;
And virtues even sufficient to atone
For all the ills the ungrateful world has done,
Where several factions, several int'rests sway,   100
And that is still i'th'right who gains the day;
Howe'er they differ, this they all must grant, }
Your form and mind, no one perfection want,   }
Without all angel, and within all saint.   }

    The murmuring world till now divided lay,
Vainly debating whom they should obey,
Till you great Cæsar's offspring blessed our isle,

The differing multitudes to reconcile;
Thus stiff-necked Israel in defiance stood,
Till they beheld the Prophet of their God;   110
Who from the Mount with dazling brightness came,
And eyes all shining with celestial flame;
Whose awful looks, dispelled each rebel thought,
And to a just compliance, the wild nations brought.

A Pindaric Poem to the Reverend Doctor Burnet, on the Honour he did me of Enquiring after me and my Muse

I

When old Rome's candidates aspired to fame,
    And did the peoples suffrages obtain
For some great consul, or a Cæsar's name;
    The victor was not half so pleased and vain,
As I, when given the honour of your choice,
And preference had in that one single voice;
    That voice, from whence immortal wit still flows;
Wit that at once is solemn all and sweet,
    Where noblest eloquence and judgment shows
The inspiring mind illustrious, rich, and great;   10
A mind that can inform your wond'rous pen
    In all that's perfect and sublime:
And with an art beyond the wit of men,
    On whate'er theme, on whate'er great design,
It carries a commanding force, like that of writ divine.

II

With pow'rful reasoning dressed in finest sense,
    A thousand ways my soul you can invade,
And spite of my opinions weak defence,
    Against my will, you conquer and persuade.
Your language soft as love, betrays the heart,   20

95

And at each period fixes a resistless dart,
   While the fond list'ner, like a maid undone,
   Inspired with tenderness she fears to own;
In vain essays her freedom to regain:
The fine ideas in her soul remain,
And please, and charm, even while they grieve and pain.

III

But yet how well this praise can recompense
For all the welcome wounds (before) you'd given!
   Scarce any thing but you and Heaven
   Such grateful bounties can dispense,   30
As that eternity of life can give;
So famed by you my verse eternally shall live:
Till now, my careless Muse no higher strove
T'enlarge her glory, and extend her wings;
   Than underneath Parnassus grove,
To sing of shepherds, and their humble love;
But never durst, like Cowley tune her strings,
   To sing of heroes and of kings.
But since by an authority divine,
She is allowed a more exalted thought;   40
She will be valued now as current coin;
Whose stamp alone gives it the estimate,
Though out of an inferior metal wrought.

IV

   But oh! if from your praise I feel
   A joy that has no parallel!
   What must I suffer when I cannot pay
   Your goodness, your own generous way?
And make my stubborn Muse your just commands obey.
   My Muse that would endeavour fain to glide
With the fair prosperous gale, and the full driving tide,   50
But loyalty commands with pious force,
   That stops me in the thriving course,

The breeze that wafts the crowding nations o'er,
    Leave me unpitied far behind
    On the forsaken barren shore,
To sigh with Echo, and the murmuring wind;
While all the inviting prospect I survey,
With melancholy eyes I view the plains,
Where all I see is ravishing and gay,
And all I hear is mirth in loudest strains;   60
Thus while the chosen seed possess the Promised Land,
    I like the excluded Prophet stand,
    The fruitful happy soil can only see,
    But am forbid by Fates decree
To share the triumph of the joyful victory.

V

'Tis to your pen, great Sir, the nation owes
For all the good this mighty change has wrought;
'Twas that the wondrous method did dispose,
Ere the vast work was to perfection brought.
Oh strange effect of a seraphic quill!   70
    That can by unperceptable degrees
Change every notion, every principle
    To any form, its great dictator please:
The sword a feeble power, compared to that,
    And to the nobler pen subordinate;
And of less use in bravest turns of state:
While that to blood and slaughter has recourse,
This conquers hearts with soft prevailing force:
So when the wiser Greeks o'ercame their foes,
It was not by the barbarous force of blows.   80
When a long ten years fatal war had failed,
With luckier wisdom they at last assailed,
Wisdom and counsel which alone prevailed.
Not all their numbers the famed town could win,
'Twas nobler stratagem that let the conquerour in.

Though I the wond'rous change deplore,
  That makes me useless and forlorn,
  Yet I the great design adore,
Though ruined in the universal turn.
Nor can my indigence and lost repose,   90
Those meagre furies that surround me close,
  Convert my sense and reason more
  To this unprecedented enterprise,
  Than that a man so great, so learn'd, so wise,
The brave achievement owns and nobly justifies.
  'Tis you, great Sir, alone, by Heaven preserved,
  Whose conduct has so well the nation served,
  'Tis you that to posterity shall give
  This ages wonders, and its history.
And great Nassau shall in your annals live   100
  To all futurity.
  Your pen shall more immortalize his name,
That even his own renowned and celebrated fame.

Notes

The Golden Age. The French original has not been identified. l.163: 'first rate of man' man in his earliest (and superior) condition.

On a Juniper-Tree, cut down to make Busks. Busks 'strip[s] of wood... passed down the front of a corset, and used to stiffen and support it. Formerly... applied to the whole corset' (OED). l.53 This line completed the couplet when the poem was first published in Rochester's *Poems upon Several Occasions* (1680), but was omitted from the 1684 version.

On the Death of Mr. Grinhil, the Famous Painter. John Greenhill (*c*.1644-76), famous portrait painter. Among his works are canvasses of Charles II, James, Duke of York, the poet Cowley, and William Cartwright, the actor. His life became irregular, and he died at his lodgings after falling into a gutter on his way home from the Vine Tavern.

A Ballad on Mr. J.H. to Amoret, asking why I was so sad. J.H. John Hoyle (*c*.1641-92), lawyer of Gray's Inn and Behn's lover in the 1670s, to whom she addressed a number of her poems. Amoret is thought to be Behn's friend, the celebrated actress Elizabeth Barry (*c*.1685-1713), who acted in several of her plays.

Song. Love Armed. The one poem of Behn's that has been frequently anthologized. It first appeared in her play, *Abdelazer* (1677).

To Mr. Creech (under the Name of Daphnis) on his Excellent Translation of Lucretius. Thomas Creech (1659-1700), fellow of All Souls', Oxford, who became a distinguished translator of classical writers. Lucretius (*c*.99-*c*.55 BC), author of the great didactic poem, *De Rerum Natura* (On the Nature of Things). He was a firm believer in the Greek philosopher Epicurus's insistence that mankind dispel superstition and anxiety through reliance on the senses and on cause and effect. l.77: 'Thirsis' Thomas Sprat (1635-1713), Bishop of Rochester, Dean of Westminster, fellow of Wadham College, Oxford, and author of the *History of The Royal Society of London* (1677). l.80: 'Cowley' Abraham Cowley (1618-67), the greatest poet of his day. l.90: 'Strephon' the famous poet and libertine, John Wilmot, Earl of Rochester (1647-80), who went to Wadham aged twelve and was created MA at fourteen. l.130: 'disticks' plural of distich, pair of verse lines, couplets.

To Mrs. W. Mrs. W. Ann Wharton (*c*.1632-85), Rochester's niece, who married Thomas Wharton (afterwards first Marquis of Wharton). Like Behn she had written her own 'Elegy on the Death of the Earl of Rochester'; and, prompting Behn's reply here, 'To Mrs. A. Behn, on what she Writ on the Earl of Rochester' (published 1693).

The Return and *On a Copy of Verses.* 'Amyntas' John Hoyle (see note above on 'A Ballad on Mr. J.H.').

To My Lady Morland at Tunbridge. Lady Morland Carola, daughter of Sir Roger Harsnett, second wife of Sir Samuel Morland. She died in 1674 aged twenty-two. A shorter version of the poem appeared in the *Muses Mercury* (1707) entitled 'To Mrs. Harsenet, on the Report of a Beauty, which she went to see at Church'. ('Mrs.' was a courtesy title). Tunbridge Wells, in Kent, was a fashionable watering-place frequented by royalty and nobility.

The Disappointment. This poem, which enjoyed considerable popularity, was sent to John Hoyle with a letter in which Behn anxiously encourages him to repudiate grave scandals concerning his private life. Hoyle (in common with other libertines of the day) was thought to indulge in both homosexual and heterosexual activity. The theme of impotence was a familiar one, the source being in the Roman poet Ovid's *Amores*, III, vi.

On a Locket of Hair. For Sir R.O. Summers proposes 'either Sir Richard Okeover, of Okeover, Staffs, knighted...[in] 1665; or Sir Richard Osbaldeston on Hunmanby, York, knighted [in] 1681'.

A Letter to a Brother of the Pen in Tribulation. Possibly addressed to fellow playwright Edward Ravenscroft (c.1640-1707). A 'tub' (l.6) is a 'sweating-tub' (see Behn's note in text) to which victims of venereal disease were subjected for a cure. To call the tub's occupant a 'tabernacler' (l.2) involves a comic allusion to 'structures temporarily used during the rebuilding of churches destroyed by the Fire of London in 1666' (OED); 'pusillage' (l.20) 'pusill' is a variant of 'pucelle', a maid (OED). Thus Behn ironically alludes to the addressee's virginity; 'coddling' (l.40)   gently boiling, stewing, with the further comic sense of nursing oneself excessively as an invalid.

To Lysander, who made some Verses and *To Lysander, on some Verses he writ.*   Lysander here is probably John Hoyle.

To the Honourable Edward Howard.   The Six Days Adventure; or, The New Utopia was produced at the Duke's Theatre in 1671, and printed the same year. Summers thinks it the best of Howard's comedies, although it was poorly received. The author justified himself vigorously in a lengthy preface. 'Ben' (l.5) and 'Great Johnson' (l.33) refer to Ben Jonson (1572?-1637). The comparisons in Howard's favour are with Jonson's *Epicene or the Silent Woman.* ll.15-19 refer to the *Utopia* (1516) of Sir Thomas More. ll.21-24 are difficult. They suggest that if Howard charitably errs in giving fine plays to an age which is incapable of appreciating them, that is not to say that the plays themselves are at fault, but rather the age's own lack of judgement. l.82 'Sir Graves' and 'Peacock' are characters in *The New Utopia.* ll.87-88 refer to Howard's *The Woman's Conquest*, performed the previous year, where the Amazons are shown vindicating themselves in victory over their neighbours, the Scythians.

A Paraphrase on Ovid's Epistle of Oenone to Paris.   A free translation from Ovid's *Heroides* (or *Epistulae*), letters of legendary heroines to their lovers, or husbands. They are studies in love from a woman's standpoint, in this case a woman betrayed and deserted. Oenone was a nymph of Mount Ida, beloved by the Trojan Paris before his abduction of Helen.

A Pindaric to Mr. P. who sings finely. Summers conjectures that this could be
addressed to the composer, Henry Purcell, who sang counter-tenor, or
possibly a relation of his who sang at the coronation of James II. Duffy,
The Passionate Shepherdess, p.142, suggests Daniel Purcell, Henry's brother.

A Pastoral to Mr. Stafford. Camilla was a maiden warrior who appears in Virgil's
Aeneid. She is killed when taking the lead in a cavalry engagement opposing
the forces of Aeneas (see Book XI). John Stafford translated this episode
for Dryden's *Sylvae: or, the Second Part of Poetical Miscellanies* (1685). l.16
'cale' Summers glosses this as an Irish word meaning hard (not in OED).
ll.62 ff. 'his noble father...Stafford's story': William Howard, Viscount
Stafford (1614-80), imprisoned in the Tower (1678) with other Catholic
peers after Titus Oates – the fabricator of the supposed Popish Plot to kill
Charles II and put his brother on the throne – had laid his 'evidence'
against them. Stafford suffered execution in a dignified manner on Tower
Hill. Oates was later found guilty of perjury.

Ovid to Julia. A Letter. Ovid (43 BC – AD 18) was banished from Rome in AD 8.
He attributed this to a poem he had written (doubtlessly the immoral *Ars
Amatoria,* or 'Art of Love'), and to some offence he had caused. The latter
was probably some kind of relationship with Julia, the profligate daughter
of the Emperor Augustus. (The subject is treated in Ben Jonson's play, *The
Poetaster.*) For possible contemporary allusions see Todd, *Works,* I, 412-3,
fn 63.

To Damon. Damon is possibly the dramatist, Edward Ravenscroft. See Duffy,
The Passionate Shepherdess, 128.

To Alexis in Answer to his Poem against Fruition. Written in reply to a copy of
verses which immediately precede it in *Lycidus,* entitled 'A Poem against
fruition written on the reading in Mountain's Essay: By Alexis'. The refer-
ence is to Montaigne's (1533-92) *Essays,* II, XV.

On Desire. A Pindaric. l.27: 'propension' inclination. l.88: 'calenture' fever,
delirium.

On a Pin that hurt Amintas' Eye. Amintas is John Hoyle.

A Letter to the Earl of Kildare. The second wife of John Fitzgerald, 18th Earl of
Kildare, proved to be the rich and beautiful Elizabeth, eldest daughter of
the 1st Earl of Ranelagh, rather than the 'Moll Howard' against whom
Behn inveighs. Summers suggests the name of Lady Margaret Howard,
sister to the Earl of Carlisle, who was notorious for her intrigues. l.18 'D—
set' is the poet and wit Charles Sackville (1638-1706), 6th Earl of Dorset.

To Mrs. Price. Identified as the actress Emily Price, who played in Behn's *Sir
Patient Fancy* (1678).

A Poem Humbly Dedicated to...Catherine, Queen Dowager. l.38: 'perjuries' the
anti-Catholic fanatic, Titus Oates, at the height of his influence had gone so

far as to accuse the Queen of intending to poison her husband.

To Henry Higden.   Higden was a well-known wit, a lawyer of the Middle Temple, who moved in the best and liveliest society. He published *A Modern Essay on the Tenth Satire of Juvenal* in 1687. l.56 'cullied' is slang, or a colloquial word; a cully was 'one who is cheated or imposed upon...a dupe, gull; one easily deceived or taken in; a silly fellow, simpleton' (OED). Behn could have any or all of these meanings in mind. l.85: 'Judah's king'   Solomon, traditionally thought to be the author of Ecclesiastes.

On the Death of E. Waller, Esq..   The poet Edmund Waller (1606-87). l.20: 'Sacharissa'   Lady Dorothy Sidney, whom Waller courted without success, the cruel but fair mistress of his love poetry. l.54: 'Generous Nine'   the Muses.

A Congratulatory Poem to Her Sacred Majesty Queen Mary and *A Pindaric Poem to the Reverend Doctor Burnet*.   See comments in the Introduction.